MW00830212

A Word to the
ABUSED

VICTOR M. JACKSON

@2024 by Victor M. Jackson

Uncaused Publishing
Orlando, FL

Printed in the United States of America

All rights reserved. No part of this publication may be reproduced, stored in a retrieval system, or transmitted in any form or by any means – for example, electronic, photocopy, recording – without the prior written permission of the publisher. The only exception is brief quotations in printed reviews.

Jackson, Victor M.
A Word to the Abused: An encouragement to those who have endured trauma, offense, and abuse.

ISBN: 979-8-9898982-3-7

This book is dedicated to every reader who hasn't had the words to express what they have been through. I pray that these words help you to find your voice.

ALSO BY VICTOR M. JACKSON

A Word to the Broken

CONTENTS

Preface 9

1. Living on What's Left 13

2. The War Between Trauma & Transition 39

3. Prisoners of Offense 65

4. Mind Over Manna 87

5. Wasted Wounds? 101

6. The Language of Scars 123

7. The Force of the Future 137

8. The Bones of a Dreamer 157

About the Author 173

PREFACE

A *Word to the Broken* has impacted lives around the world. The hunger and the healing that has taken place in people have forever changed me. I have wept with these readers. I have shared tears of hurt and tears of healing with our readers. *A Word to the Abused* is book 2 in the "A Word to the Broken" series. This book takes a deep dive into the healing journey that many of you are on. The purpose of this book is simply to encourage you on your healing journey. The intention of this book is not to replace your daily devotions with God or to interfere with your visitations to your professional counselor. This book is simply an encouragement for you to continue on your journey of healing. This book desires to come alongside you to comfort and uplift you in the journey. I do believe that this book is a must-read. It was born out of necessity. There is so much to say about brokenness. I needed a second book. There is so much to say about abuse. I am writing a third book.

There are four intricate parts of humanity that I aim to minister to in this book (heart, soul, mind, and strength). These are essential parts of you that God desires. We must love the Lord with our heart, mind, soul, and strength. Chapters 1 and 2 deal with the heart of the matter. Chapters 3, 4, and 5 deal with the mind. These parts of a human life are essential to align with God and accomplish his will for our lives. I am shifting your perspective and positioning you to walk in victory in these areas. In chapters 6, I attempt to minister to the depths of the soul. Chapters 7 and 8 impart strength to the reader. This book will help propel you into your future. It is time.

Allow this book to challenge you and to heal you. Don't run from a challenge. Finish the book. Don't run from your healing. Finish the book. I know that many will be healed and transformed by the power of God. Paul's desire for the church in Thessalonica was that God would sanctify them wholly through their spirit, soul, and body. My desire in this book is that it reaches your spirit and ministers to your mind, will, and emotions. I pray that these words do not just stay on the inside but also manifest outwardly through your actions and behaviors. I pray that you grow in your habits and the fruit of the Spirit. When they see your good works, others will glorify your Father, which is in heaven.

I thank my wife, Luisa, for supporting me in this endeavor. My daughter Mia and my son James Asher have been such a strength to me. Family and friends, thank you. Bible Center of Orlando and the Bible Center churches, thank you for covering me in your prayers.

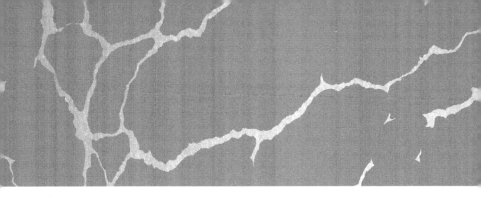

Manipulative people will intentionally hurt you and then make you feel guilty for being a victim. You do not have to endure abuse to prove your love. Abuse is "abnormal use." It's not normal. Be set free from that mental and emotional bondage; you are not crazy for avoiding abuse and toxicity. God is about to give you victory. God is for you. You will be healed and overcome.

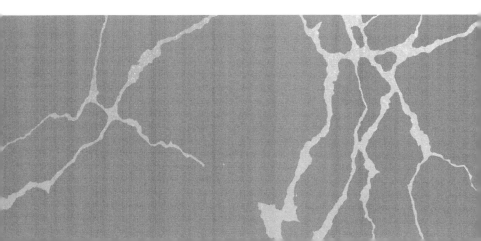

1

LIVING ON WHAT'S LEFT

The Lord said to Abram, after Lot had separated from him,
"Lift up your eyes and look from the place where you are,
northward and southward and eastward and westward, for all the
land that you see I will give to you and to your offspring forever.

GENESIS 13:14-15 ESV

You have lost so much. It is difficult to put into words. You are stuck with the feeling of loss. You thought that you would have that person in your life forever, but now you are grieving over everything that you have lost. You have invested years into that relationship, but it's gone now. You gave your best to that marriage, but now it is in shambles. You gave your best years to that company, but they let you go. You have tried to move on with a smile because you do not want to seem bitter. It appears that after you suffer loss, the "happiness police" are standing over you. They watch your every move like vultures to see if any sign of bitterness may be creeping into your spirit. The vultures do not offer a helping hand for you to get up and recover. No, they are vultures. They pick at the wound and remind you and others that you are not perfect. They stand on the poles of divinity, watching over the streets of humanity and mocking and pecking at anything struggling. You hide under fig leaves to escape their gaze. These fig leaves did not work for Adam and Eve, neither will it work for you. Welcome to humanity. You are not a robot; you are a human. Robots do not bleed, but humans do. Whenever we become wounded, the vultures circle. They can identify pain from a mile away. They circle pain, but they flee from any sign of joy. Attracted to death but intimidated by life.

You put on your smile and your best face because you do not want to be labeled as that "bitter" person. You cannot even say, "I am not bitter." Because the first thing that the "happiness police" tell you is, "Only bitter people say that they are not bitter." When you are hurt, it seems that you cannot win. After accepting defeat, you have learned how to live with the labels. You are not the first person to be labeled. Blind Bartimaes. The woman with the issue. Simon the leper. People have defined you by what has happened to you. You have had to learn to live with the label. People have placed a label on you so that they can live with themselves. Putting labels on others is a manipulative way to not accept accountability in their own lives. Slowly the label has become your identity. You have worn the label for so long that you don't even remember who you were before it was attached to you. If someone attached a label to you, they believe they own you. You only put labels on things that you own or control. They feel that they alone can determine your value. You are not anyone's property. You are a child of God. The problem is that you have begun to define yourself by what happened. You have welcomed the label because it is all you have left. Instead of the label being attached to us, now *we* are attached to the label.

You have tried to move on but cannot ignore the losses. You gave your best years to that church, but something went wrong. You gave your best years to that relationship. It's gone. You gave your life to that company, but something unexpected happened. You feel ashamed. You feel like a fool because you gave so much of yourself. Thoughts of revenge flood your mind. It is difficult to heal in front of the people that broke you. Everyone is watching you, the abused. But no one is watching the abuser. The vultures are watching you, the "offended." But everyone is ignoring the actions of the offender. They are watching you and how you are handling your trauma. But no one is watching the person that caused the trauma. Unfortunately, the world has made being offended worse than being the offender. If you are the offender, you will be protected. If you are offended, you are shunned. If you are the offender, you receive support. If you are offended, you receive rejection. Yes, we know that being offended is the "Bait of Satan," the question is, why are saints and family the ones that are setting the traps for little children? Focusing on the offended instead of the offender's actions is to protect the system instead of the victim. Jesus revealed to the disciples his attitude towards the offender,

Whosoever therefore shall humble himself as this little child, the same is greatest in the kingdom of heaven. And whoso shall receive one such little child in my name receiveth me. But whoso shall offend one of these little ones which believe in me, it were better for him that a millstone were hanged about his neck, and that he were drowned in the depth of the sea. Woe unto the world because of offences! for it must needs be that offences come; but woe to that man by whom the offence cometh (Matthew 18:4-7 KJV)!

This Scripture reveals the severity in which God sees the offender. How did the world and church systems get this scripture backward? The offender must repent, and the offended must heal and move on. You were molested as a child, and somehow, they claimed it was your fault. Your body was still developing; you were too young to process these emotions yourself. But you were forced to process it alone. The family didn't defend you. Leadership didn't defend you. The company didn't defend you. The people in the church didn't defend you. But rest assured, God is going to defend you. This Scripture in Matthew is no excuse to live offended because that is a miserable life. Process the pain. Grieve over the pain. Process how much damage they have caused. Shun bitterness. Flee revenge. Contemplate the years that you have lost. Then, finally, forgive and move on. This book will help you heal and move forward because your best days are ahead of you. You are not crazy like they said you were. You just wanted to be heard. I hear you. No, really, I hear you, and more importantly, God hears you. It is difficult to move on. It seems like everyone else has moved on as if nothing happened, but you are frozen. Those closest to you have told you to move on, but you cannot stop replaying the trauma in your mind. Friends will grieve with you for a little while, but after your pain passes the time limit that they have placed upon you, friends can disappear quickly. The trauma piles up. Betrayal after betrayal. You wonder what is real and what is fake. You just don't know, and you just don't care anymore. You are frozen. You exercise, but you feel frozen. You talk to your therapist, but you feel frozen. You are taking medication, but you feel frozen. You found a new church, friends, job, and city but are still frozen. You have discovered that a change of scenery is not enough to change your soul. It is a step in the right direction of healing. But your soul was broken by man; therefore, it can only be restored by God. You need God's help whenever you are frozen. This is one of the effects of a traumatic experience; you can freeze. It can stunt your growth mentally, emotionally, and spiritually. Whenever you are tired of fighting and tired of running, you freeze. You need the Holy Spirit's warmth when trying to unfreeze. You need God's fire to burn in your heart. You need His Word in your life because dealing with trauma is draining. You have given up trying to explain your pain because a narcissist will always convince you that your pain is your fault. They ask questions like: "Why did you make me hit you?" They say crazy things like, "If your skirt weren't so tight, they wouldn't have raped you." "Why did you go with me?" They share ridiculous things like, "They wouldn't have abused you if you didn't go to that event." Wrong place, wrong time, they say. Why didn't you do this? Why didn't you do that? People focus on the event and the surroundings without offering help or nourishment to the soul. The vultures pick apart every social media post, hoping for a hint of bitterness from you. The "happiness police" have secret meetings to dissect every phrase and emoji to ensure you are not referencing the vultures or the people, places, and things that have harmed you. The thing about the "happiness police" is that they are not happy. They are so miserable with their problems that they project their issues upon you. They are sorting through their trauma, but instead of dealing with it, they spend their energy on you. They spend their energy conniving, tearing down, mocking, manipulating, and even hoping that they turn you into the same miserable version of themselves. So much energy is spent trying to destroy you, and they do not have any time and energy to build something beautiful for themselves. Pray for them. God needs to heal them as well. They may not even recognize what they are doing because they do not realize they need to heal and recover. Pastors, leaders, and parents are ciphering through their trauma. Some pastors were once little church kids that were dropped off at a neighbor's house, and it was there that they saw porn for the first time. They were touched and raped, so now they project their anger on their saints. They felt defenseless in the past, so they acted macho and invincible in the present. They haven't been the same since. My heart breaks for humanity. We need to treat one another better. I have witnessed the pain that leaders have caused. But I have also witnessed the pain that congregations have caused on leaders. I have witnessed CEO's and founders pushed out of their companies by greedy and conspiring board members. Where is the love? Abuse in any fashion is wrong. Abuse towards leadership and abuse from leadership cannot be tolerated. I have seen people intentionally hurt Pastors and Pastor's wives because of jealousy. I weep writing this. I have seen young saints treated with malice because of their unique gifts. I have seen employees taken advantage of. God, heal us all. I am interceding for every leader and every follower. Every reader that is reading this book, I am praying for you. We are bleeding on one another. Abuse is not an authority issue. It is a humanity issue. Anyone can be misused. Just because you were misused, it does not permit you to misuse others. I weep over your life and what you have suffered. Some parents project their trauma upon their kids. We are supposed to honor our father and mother, but it is tough to honor someone who has not nourished you. The reward for nourishment is honor. But if a parent is poisoning the child, they are not quick to honor the parent. No nourishment, no honor. No matter what title a person has in your life (pastor, parent, etc.), you will not naturally give honor unless you have received nourishment from them. Children grow up wanting to honor someone, but their parents have only tried to sabotage them or destroy them with drugs and malnourishment. These children grow up, and instead of honoring their parents, they honor their craft. They honor their gift. They become workaholics and incredibly gifted individuals because they placed their honor on their craft and abilities. If you research highly gifted and successful people, it is interesting to see their traumatic childhoods. These individuals become performance-driven and doers. They know how to do but do not know how to be. Tension arises whenever a parent who has abandoned or abused their child begins to demand honor. No nourishment, no honor. I am not saying that not giving honor is right, but I am describing what happens in human nature when things get distorted. When a parent does not function properly in their biblical role (nourishment), it is difficult for the child to do as well (honor). Whenever proper nourishment starts, then proper honor will follow. It is the authority's responsibility to initiate proper nourishment; it is not the child's responsibility. If a parent gives proper nourishment, but the child refuses to honor them. That is called rebellion. Children have a responsibility to align themselves biblically. There is an interesting scripture concerning this concept; Thou shalt not seethe a kid in his mother's milk (Exodus 23:19). You shall not boil a young goat in their mother's milk. This is an Old Testament principle: The place of nourishment should never become the place of destruction. The milk that feeds the goat should never be the milk that is used to boil the goat. Family and churches are supposed to be safe places of nourishment for an individual. But it is toxic whenever the place of nourishment becomes the place of harm, abuse, and destruction. People begin to honor jobs, careers, and relationships. But they will not be fulfilled until they honor God. Honoring God will fix our relationships with one another and our relationship with our craft. Honoring God will help us to honor humanity. I have seen relationships healed and restored whenever God enters the equation. Your relationship with your family and even leaders can be healed if both sides are willing to honor God. Anything that is not in alignment biblically is simply dysfunctional. We are all a work in progress. Be gracious with one another. As you have children of your own and lead your own causes, you will understand their humanity a bit more. No excuses. But humanity is very complex because everyone is sorting through some type of trauma. There is no excuse for any form of abuse, but we must understand these patterns so that we can overcome them and help others to overcome them. We have to stop the cycle of pain. We are bleeding upon people that did not hurt us. Now your new relationships, new pastor, and new boss have to deal with your anger towards them, although they didn't do anything to you. You are suspicious of joy and purpose; therefore, you are irritated whenever you are in its presence. You have become cynical. Happy people have begun to bother you. If you see one more "happy" couple on social media, you are going to throw your phone at the wall! You are tired.

You are tired of playing defense all the time. You have repeatedly said, "I'm sorry," for no reason. You tell the cashier, "I'm sorry" for giving them your money. Someone hurts *you*, and you say, "I'm sorry." You speak the words, "I'm sorry" five times a day because you are fearful of becoming hardened. You are scared to become exactly what they think of you. You have come to the place you would rather be run over and walked upon as long as they do not accuse you of being mad or bitter. You cannot be bitter. You must not be bitter. Bitterness is a seducing spirit that will try to turn you into the person that hurt you. But you aren't bitter; you are *tired.* You have bottled up so much emotion. It is taking everything in you to manage it. You have no energy for the future because so much has been spent managing the past. Here you are 10 years later, 30 years later, and 1 year later, still calculating everything you have lost. Whenever you leave your home, you make sure that you greet the "happiness police" with a smile as you continue to pretend that all is well. But all is not well! You gave your best years to that church; how could it end like this? You gave that business, marriage, team, and friend many years. The people that you praised with you are now your enemies and stand against you. The word Judah in Hebrew means "praise." When translated into Greek, the word Judah is "Judas." There are some people that will Judah you to Judas you. They Judah with you now, but they Judas (betray) you later. Praisers can become betrayers when they are not healed. We need healing in this hour.

You ask yourself, "How did I get here?" The losses are incalculable. This hurts. How can you move on after something so traumatic? You were treated less than human. Animals are treated better. You still cry over what happened. You have dreams of defending yourself at night. You wake up with tears. You are in a cold sweat; you go back to sleep.

You have nightmares of them hurting you again. You wake up with tears again. How do you move on after these losses?

You must learn to live on what's left. What you have left is more significant than anything that you have lost. You must believe that the future is greater than the past. Stop making people your entire book whenever they were only supposed to be a single chapter. You have tried to end your own story too early. You are arriving at the best part of your story; do not throw the book away before you get to the best part. Every hero must have a tragedy. Clark Kent was abandoned as a child. Bruce Wayne was stuck in a cave with bats. Peter Parker lost his uncle. Every hero has a tragedy in their story. The tragedy makes the hero. I know those are fictional heroes, but we have a real hero who went through trauma for us: Jesus Christ.

There is no masterpiece without a mess. Tragedies give birth to heroes. Pain is what makes them unique and sets them apart from the crowd. The heartache provides the person with meaning. Getting up and living for a higher purpose can become a motivating factor. Today is where your story shifts. The abuse did not kill you. The trauma does not define you. The offense is not in charge of your destiny. This is the climax of your story. Today is the most important day of your life. As long as you have something left, you have hope. You can thrive on what you have left. No need to spend another moment obsessing over who hurt you. No need to plot your revenge. There is no need to spend more energy hating them because it takes energy away from your healing.

Let's be honest; they won that round. No shame in admitting that. They triumphed in that chapter. But the rest of the book belongs to you! *A Word to the Abused* will not highlight your enemies or those who tried to destroy you. This book will teach you how to forgive, heal, and move on with victory. You will thrive in this chapter of your life. You are about to soar. This book will thrust you into the abundant life that Jesus Christ promised you. Your healing journey is the focus of this book. Your healing is the priority. This book was written to help you to move forward. Your story is not over. You have something left in the tank. God will use whatever you have left. Whatever you have left, God will use it to create a masterpiece. If you have something left, that is just the beginning. Holding on to the pain of what you lost will make you bitter. Holding on to the power of what you have left will make you better. What you lost is for the past. What you have left is for the future.

Abram found himself in a dilemma. God was increasing him, but he did not have room to grow because of Lot. Abram needed more room for the promise of God to be fulfilled in his life. Sometimes, whenever God wants to elevate you, he will allow some friction to get you to separate from the thing holding you back from your purpose. Abram sees that the friction intensifies, so Abram tells his nephew to choose a portion of land to dwell in. He told him that he would live on whatever land was left. The Bible says that Lot chose all the plains of Jordan. Abram was forced to dwell on whatever land was left. Abram trusted God so much that he was willing to live on what was left. He believed that whatever he lost, God could multiply what he had left. Abram had a Lot. *We* have our "Lot in Life."

Life knows how to take from us. All of us are forced to live with our "Lot in Life." A person's "lot in life" refers to fortune or misfortune determined by fate, chance, and luck. A "lot" was a token, often a marked stone cast with others, like dice, to determine an outcome by sheer chance. Your lot in life is simply the circumstances you must live with. Living with something that you have little control over. Abram had to deal with his "Lot," which meant he had to deal with losses. But Abram dared to live on what's left because he understood that hell can never take everything from you. Hell has to leave something behind. The devil cannot take everything; there must be something left. Abram was willing to have faith in what he had left. He believed that the promise of God could be completed in what remained. He made peace with what he lost because he believed that he could live prosperously on whatever land was left.

No matter what you have been through in your life. No matter what you have lost. You must have the courage to live on what's left. God told Abram, "Look from the place that you are." You must learn to look from your lack. Because from your lack, you can launch. You may be lacking, but God is preparing you to launch. God told him to look where he was and to look all around him. God told him he would possess the land from whatever he had left. You can possess the land from what is left. The promise will be fulfilled from what you have left, not from what you have lost. Abram was willing to live on what was left because what was left was sufficient for the promise of God to be fulfilled. Again, hell cannot take everything from you. Whatever is left, God is willing to work a miracle. Whatever is left, God is willing to open a door. Whatever is left, God is willing to heal. God is willing to fulfill his word. You have something left that God is willing to work with.

When you're walking through life, you begin to think about everything you have lost. You start to feel like you do not have enough. You think that you can't live on the little that you have, but God is saying, "Look from the place that you are. I'm willing to do something with what you have left." Your heart has been broken; bring that damaged heart to God because he is willing to use whatever is left. No matter how bruised and bloody it is, he wants to use your heart. Bring to God whatever is left because he will use it for his glory. Although Lot chose all the plain of Jordan, God brought the promise to Abram out of the land that was left.

We must have the courage to live on what's left because it's sufficient to bring you into what God has for you. It's so easy to weep and mourn over what you lost. What you lost is connected to your past, but what you have left is connected to your future. If you lose it, that means that you can live without it. If you lose it, it is not needed for your destiny. What you have left is sufficient to become everything God has called you to be. You have something left. God brought his word to pass in Abram's life from the place that he was.

I want everyone reading this to look at the place that you are and realize that the promise is coming out of where you are. You have enough. God told the church in Philadelphia, "There's an open door set before you. Because you have a little strength" (Revelation 3:8). You just have a little strength left. You have a little faith left. You still have my name. You still have my word. A door is opening because you still have something left. You don't need a lot of strength for an open door. You just need to have something left. God is willing to open a door with the little you have left. You don't need a lot of faith. You still have God's word, and you still have His name. You have just enough for an open door. God's doors are opening for you based on what you have. He defines you by what you have presently, not by what you have lost. You still have a little strength, which is enough for a God door. Man's doors can close on you whenever they consider what you lost, but God doors open for you because of what you have left.

It makes me think of a painter named Terry Redlin from South Dakota. Terry Redlin was known for his incredible painting skills and how he portrayed the shadows and the sun upon the waters. He truly adored wildlife and anything to do with nature. He could paint a picture and tell a story using five different canvases to paint a story's progression. Painting a young man becoming older. Watching the progression of a young man playing with toys and then becoming a soldier. The young man is then being deployed, and his parents are getting older. The young man dying on duty and a flag being brought to the parent's home. He was a master at painting stories in multiple canvases.

But Terry Redlin's dream was not to become a painter. He always wanted to be a forest ranger. He was preparing as a young child to be a forest ranger, but he had an unfortunate accident. He had an accident where he lost one of his limbs. Because of the injury, he became confined to a wheelchair. The dream of becoming a forest ranger was lost forever. But out of his loss, he discovered his gift for painting. He discovered his gift with what he had left. His loss forced him to discover his gift.

He lost something, but he found something. Anytime you lose something, you find something. He lost the dream of becoming a park ranger, but he found his calling to be an artist. He lost his leg, but he realized that God could use what he had left. He lost a leg, but he found his gift with his hands. His gift would be discovered and flourish out of what he had left. He impacted the world with what he had left.

I saw the chair he would paint in; it was on a swivel. It was a beautiful chair. There was paint all over it, drops of paint of all different colors. It was in his handicap that he found his gift. His handicap helped him to discover the gift that would coincidentally help him to heal internally and emotionally. God will heal you with whatever you have left. In his loss, he learned to value what he had left. It was what Terry had left that caused him to discover his gift. It was what he had left that caused him to make an impact on his city. They made a whole museum for him in South Dakota. People come from all across the world to see his art. He learned to thrive in what he had left. He could have become bitter and mean-spirited out of his pain. But his injury became his asset. His adversity became his advantage. His hurt became his help. His trial ushered in his triumph. Redlin's gift is still impacting lives today. Look at what God can do when someone becomes thankful that they have something left. A more extraordinary dream will arise out of what you have left. It will go beyond anything that you lost. How many of you have been beating yourself up over that lost dream? All the wasted years. You still ruminate over the things that you have suffered in your life. God is going to redeem the time. It's time to look from where you are because what you have left is where you'll find your gift. It makes me think of David. God told the prophet to go to Jesse's house because he found a man after his own heart. Samuel goes to Jesse's house, and he does not find a man; he finds a boy. But there was a man in the boy. God would later raise up a giant, to bring the man out of the boy. Your giants in life are working for you. It will produce something out of you that you did not know that you had within you. David thought he was a shepherd, but his giant showed him that there was a king within him. You thought you were rejected, but the adversity showed you that you are royalty. They did not realize what was within David because everyone underestimates the value of what's left. The prophet Samuel went to Jesse's house, and Jesse put forth his strongest sons. The first son that Jesse puts forth is Eliab, whose name means "strength of my father." Jesse wanted the prophet to anoint his strongest sons.

Samuel tried to anoint these seven sons, but the anointing wouldn't pour over them. Samuel asked Jesse, "Do you have any sons left?" (1 Samuel 16:11). Jesse says, "All we have left is David." David wasn't a part of the meeting. David wasn't invited; he was tending the sheep. They thought that there wasn't anything special about David. But Samuel said, "Go get him because the oil will be poured on the son you have left." The oil never falls on the majority. It always falls on what's left. The anointing oil came upon what was left. It didn't come on the strongest sons but on the son he had left.

What you have left is sufficient for the anointing oil to flow. What you have left is enough for the oil to anoint and set apart for God's glory. No matter how people, society, or culture has tried to count you out. What you have left is where the anointing will operate and flow from.

Abram was left with Lot's leftovers and God said, "Look from the place that you are. I'm willing to fulfill my word with it." Lot chose all the plain of Jordan, and the Bible says that Abram dwelled. He was living on what was left, but we see the promise of God coming to fruition with what he had left.

I don't know what storms you faced or trials you overcame, but you have life in your body. That means you have something left that God wants to use to help you possess the land.

There were times in my life when I lost a lot, and I would get discouraged, intimidated, afraid, and worried over all the stuff that I lost. I asked myself, "How will I recover from this?" God responded, "Look from the place that you are. You have enough left for me to fulfill my word in your life. Develop the courage to live on what's left."

I have been very open with my testimony of overcoming abuse. My story has helped others to see that there is life after physical, spiritual, mental, and sexual abuse. These unfortunate events are truly tough. It is difficult to explain to others. But I have seen many people impacted when they understand they are not alone.

I was locked in closets growing up. I was beaten severely by my stepdad. I loved my stepdad with all of my heart. What most people do not know is that when you are abused, it is very easy to forgive others. The difficulty is blaming yourself for what happened to you. I never hated my stepdad, but I did learn to hate myself. I loved and still love him, but I hated myself. I wondered what was wrong with me. He was perfect; I must be garbage. He would lock me in the closet and then take the rest of the family out to eat. He would lock me in the closet, and I would be left alone until he returned from work. He locked me in rooms, and I wouldn't be able to come out for days. Occasionally, I had to sneak in the middle of the night to grab a Pop-Tart from the pantry. I had to hide the wrappers under my toys. I learned how to take naps in the storage closet. He put a Nintendo game system in the storage closet for me to play during the day. I remember trying to comfortably fall asleep on top of dozens of dusty and empty boxes.

I would try to sleep all day in that closet for the time to pass. To this day I can fall asleep anywhere at any time because of this experience. I loved him, I tried my best to be perfect, so I would not get in trouble. But for some reason, my presence was irritating to him. I had very low self-esteem. It is difficult to develop confidence when you are beaten for no reason daily. I had high-functioning anxiety, which led to injuries later in life when I played college basketball. My body was under constant stress. Although I had forgiven him, it took years for my body to recover because the body stores trauma. I lost a lot of my childhood. I lost a lot of time. I lost a lot of self-esteem. I tried to improve my self-esteem through basketball, but it wasn't enough. I needed something more significant. I needed someone who would never leave me or forsake me. I needed Jesus Christ to heal me. He taught me how to live on what's left. All I had was a little strength. All I had was a relationship with God. I believed that God could get glory out of what I had left. God took me under his tutelage. My Heavenly Father taught me how to love others more deeply. I forgave my stepdad. If I could forgive him, I can forgive anyone. I forgave him, and I moved on.

Because God taught me a principle, he always does more with what you have left. God gave me a ministry out of what I had left. And he has used my pain to minister to millions around the world. God is still using what I have left. God is still multiplying. The devil tried to take everything, but he couldn't. Now, God will make hell pay with what I have left. The devil is going to wish that he never touched your family. God is about to open a door with what you have left. There are examples in the Old Testament and the New Testament of what God can do in and through people who give him what's left.

There was a woman in the Old Testament that had lost her husband. Her husband was one of the sons of the prophets. After her husband died, the creditor came to take away her sons. She was a widow, and she owed a lot of money. She pleaded with the prophet Elijah to help her. She was tormented over losing her husband and potentially losing the next generation. The prophet asked her, "What do you have left in the house?" All she had left was a pot of oil (2 Kings 4:2). The prophet said, "That is all you need." What you have left is all you need for a miracle. He told her to start pouring the oil into the vessels, and the oil multiplied. Multiplication came out of what she had left. The more she poured the oil into vessels, the more the oil continued to flow. She sold the oil and was able to pay off the creditor. She could have held onto the pain of loss, but she invested her time in the oil she had left. Her answer was already in the house. Her answer to her problem was in what she had left. Your answer is in what you have left. You are looking outside for help, but God is looking at what you have left. What you have left is the source of your deliverance.

This principle is beautifully illustrated in the New Testament. In the New Testament, we can see God's ability to work with what we have left. Throughout the Gospels, Jesus healed the blind, the deaf, the lame, and the mute. These people suffered different handicaps, but it is unique how God worked with them, although they had a disability. The blind were blind, but they could still hear with their ears. The blind used what they had left of their senses to get them to Jesus.

They used whatever they had left to bridge them into a relationship with Jesus. You have something left to bring you to Jesus. They used their ears to get them into a miracle. The deaf were deaf, but they could still see with their eyes. They used what they saw to bring them to Jesus to get a miracle. They used their eyes to bring them closer to God.

The lame were lame. The lame couldn't walk, but they could see and hear. Even though they were handicapped, they used what they had left to put themselves in a position to get their miracle from Jesus. They couldn't walk, but they still had a voice to shout. They used whatever they had left. The mute couldn't speak. But they could hear, they could see, and they could touch. They used what they had left to bring them into a miracle from Jesus. God was willing to work with the senses that they had left.

If a blind man used what he had left. If a deaf man used what he had left. If a lame man used what he had left. If a mute man used what he had left. You can still use what you have left. God can still use what you have left. You have something left to bring you to Jesus. You have something left to give birth to a miracle. You have something left to get a miracle. Purpose is coming out of what you have left. Power is coming out of what you have left. Although they could have made an excuse to not pursue God, they still pursued him. Despite the inadequacy. Despite the past hurt. Despite the stigma. Despite the handicap. Despite the spiritual attack. They still saw value in what they had left. God healed them all. Don't look at your lack and say that you can't launch. Out of your lack, you are going to launch. Out of your pain, you're going to discover power. God wants to use what you have left. You just have to be willing to give it to him. He wants to work a miracle out of whatever you have left. He will use your lack to make you whole again. He is going to restore you with what remains.

Look from the place that you are. God is going to get glory in what you have left. The blind man didn't fall into a pity party. He could hear Jesus walking by, so he cried out, "Jesus, thou son of David, have mercy on me." The deaf couldn't hear anything but saw a man working miracles. They used the rest of their senses to bring them to Jesus. I can't walk, but I will use my voice to bring him to me. You have something left to get you to Jesus. Whatever has happened to you that has handicapped you spiritually, physically, emotionally, or mentally. You still have something left that God wants to use.

If you lost your son to cancer, use the memory that you have left of him and start a cancer foundation. The most outstanding philanthropic organizations were birthed out of personal pain. CEOs suffered personal losses but learned to build their lives anew with whatever they had left. You discover pain in your loss, but you discover purpose in what you have left.

I think about the people in the New Testament who were on the journey. They left the cities on foot to search for Jesus in the wilderness (Matthew 14:13). They went out on foot to follow Jesus and started their journey toward him. If you are going into the wilderness, starting that journey with food is essential.

No one knows how much food they started their journey with. But the prolonged nature of the journey began to subtract their food. They ran on foot out of the cities into the wilderness. They grabbed whatever belongings and food that they could and followed him. But the journey had taken so much from them that it began subtracting. All that they had left was five loaves and two fish. God said, "Give me what you have left because I'm willing to multiply it with what you have left." All they had left was five loaves and two fish. Jesus responded to their lack: "Bring it to me." Bring Jesus what you have that's limited. He is willing to make it into something unlimited. Bring Him what you have; that's not enough. He is willing to use it and make it more than enough. Bring Him what you have left because that's all he needs to multiply and do something you've never seen before. You can feed more with what you have left than you could have if you never suffered a loss. Multiplication will flow out of what's left.

They probably started their journey with a lot of food, but the journey began to subtract. All they had left was five loaves and two fish. In the story, it does not focus on what they lost. Neither does it focus on what they had before they started the journey. None of that mattered; the crux of the story was about what God could do with whatever you had left. He can multiply the leftovers. Those fish probably smelled. The bread was probably moldy. You don't want to show Jesus that filth; you want to hide it away from Him. But he still wants what is dirty. He wants what is expired. He wants whatever is insufficient. Because when he sees these things, he knows he is about to get glory. He is not afraid of the stench. Bring God what you have left because that's all he needs for a miracle.

How many of you started your journey with a lot of faith? You believed that God could do anything. You believed that anything could happen, but then you suffered a loss. After you had a loss in the family. After you've had setback after setback in your ministry. After you've had setbacks in your job, family, and career. After a leader or family member hurts you. After you have invested in someone and they betrayed your trust. They walked out of you. They left you whenever you needed them the most. You poured your life into them. The journey has subtracted your faith. Now, it is difficult to believe in God for great things. It's tough to believe for greatness. It's a challenge to believe in God for blessing. It's a fight to believe in anointing. It's a war to believe in a bright future. You started well, but the journey of life begins to subtract. The losses have piled up.

But if you just have a little left. If you just have a mustard seed of faith left. God is willing to use it to move a mountain. Develop the courage to live on what's left because what you have left is sufficient to feed thousands. What do you have left? Five loaves and two fishes? Just bring it to Jesus because he can use it for his glory. Moldy. Crusted. Antiquated. Old. Damaged goods. Bring it to Jesus and watch what he does. Divorced. Abused. Traumatized. Bring it to Him. Watch God work. It's not over when you have something left.

Jesus commissioned 500 people to wait in the upper room to receive the Holy Spirit. He said two words that challenge and separate the hungry from the full. All Jesus said was, "Go wait," the waiting would reveal who was hungry. He said, "Go wait in the city of Jerusalem until you are endued with power from on high" (Luke 24:49). You will receive the greatest miracle, but you must wait for it. The waiting reveals who's hungry and who's not. The waiting reveals who really wants it bad and who is just along for the journey.

He commissioned 500 people to wait in Jerusalem to be endued with power from on high (1 Corinthians 15:6). But the Bible says that only 120 people showed up. The majority left. But God poured out his Spirit on the 120 that were left. 380 walked away, but God poured out his Spirit upon those that were left. The anointing came upon those that were left. God changed the world with the 120 people that he had left. Whatever you have left, God's willing to change the world. You may not have a lot, but you have something left. Imagine if the 120 people got discouraged because 380 people left the upper room. Only 120 showed up to receive the promise of the Father. But the oil never flows on the majority. It always flows on the remnant. It always flows on what's left. 120 were left, but then in a single day 3,000 people were added to the kingdom. Where did that start? It started with God using what he had left. 3,000 people were added to the church. Sometimes, God has to subtract some things to add much more to you. He used what he had left.

The enemy attacked Job, and Job lost his family. He lost his reputation. He lost his lands. He lost his house. He lost a lot, but he still had his health. Then hell came and attacked his health, and he lost his health, but he still had his life. Hell can never take everything, and all that Job had left was his life. The only thing he had left was his life and his wife. God gave him a double portion of what he had left. There was blessing upon his life and more children from his wife. His wife wasn't happy with what they had left, but God gave her back double for her trouble. She was bitter initially. She told Job to curse God and die (Job 2:9). But her ending was beautiful (Job 42:13-15). She didn't understand the pain. But the loss was only for a chapter; her story was not over. God gave her back double. God gave Job's wife more than she could imagine. You may have been bitter initially. Perhaps you were offended against God like she was. But your story is not over. What you have left is sufficient to receive a double portion. He would not relinquish his relationship with God when everything was taken away. Don't let go of God. He is going to turn everything around for you.

Out of what's left, a miracle's coming. Out of what's left, an anointing is coming. Out of what's left, a transformation is coming. You just have to have the courage to live on what's left. Be encouraged. You have something left. Some of you may think that all you have left is mistakes. You ask yourself, "How can God use me if all I have in my hand are mistakes that I have made on the journey of trauma and heartache." If all you have left is mistakes, God will get glory out of your life. No one is perfect. You are human. Not everyone responds to trauma the same way. Maybe you lashed out or sought vengeance. Perhaps you turned to hate. There is still hope for you. God is not finished with you. It is time to come out of hiding. Be who God has called you to be. You were made in the image of God. Sin has tried to deform you. Jesus has come to conform you to His image and transform you by renewing your mind (Romans 12:1-2). Through him, you are coming out of this chapter of heartache. Let's get into the next chapter of your healing journey.

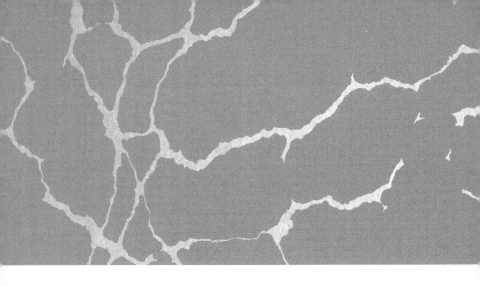

Going through excessive pain without becoming cynical or bitter is a victory within itself. Being able to smile and trust again is a victory worth rejoicing over. Rejoice in the Lord; he is your healer.

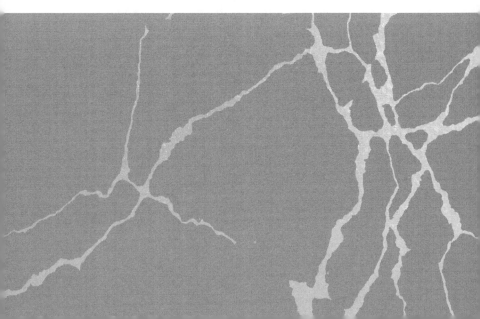

2

THE WAR BETWEEN TRAUMA & TRANSITION

The Lord said to Samuel, "How long will you grieve over Saul, since I have rejected him from being king over Israel? Fill your horn with oil, and go. I will send you to Jesse the Bethlehemite, for I have provided for myself a king among his sons." And Samuel said, "How can I go?

1 SAMUEL 16:1-2 ESV

There is an incredible story concerning the loyal Japanese soldiers from World War II. The training of these Japanese soldiers was so rigorous. They invested a lot of time in preparing for World War II. Their entire belief system was configured for this particular war. Their preparation and attention to detail was impeccable. The soldiers were commanded to go into hiding whenever Japan began to lose the war. While they were hiding, the war ended on September 2nd, 1945. These men prepared and invested so much into the war; they had no idea it was over. These soldiers, who were called holdouts, had no idea that the war was over, even after many years had gone by. Some were still dressed in war clothes for many years after the war ended. The war was over. But these soldiers were so invested in what they had been through that they could not process a new reality.

Five years passed, and many of them still believed that they were still at war. Ten years would pass, many of them still believing that they were still at war. 29 years would pass and they were still awake every day preparing for battle. Hiroo Onoda was one of the last soldiers still holding their post and fighting a war that ended 30 years prior. In 1974 a tourist encountered him and tried to persuade him that the war was over. He was still in uniform and holding his weapons with a fierce grip. He was still in war mode, not believing that the war was over. He did not believe the magazines or the newspapers. Everything was a threat to him. Finally, they flew him to Japan and convinced him that the world had moved on. After 30 years, he was finally able to live his life. These holdouts were so invested in their history that they did not know how to live in their present. Peace was a foreign concept whenever you were used to fighting so much.

We cannot blame him because many of us are living with this same experience in our own lives. God is trying to take us to new heights and new levels, but we have such an investment in the past that we do not know how to move. God is trying to move in the present, but we become paralyzed by the pain of yesterday. We become overwhelmed with today and tomorrow because so much investment has gone into the past. It is challenging to let go of your investment. You invested so much in relationships, friendship, company, and church. It is tough to let it go when you become so invested that you are a stranger to your present. You don't realize that the war is over. It's not coming back. It's over.

That there was an expiration date on your trial, but what hell wants to do is he wants to persuade your mind that you're still in a battle. You've already survived. You've already come through. You've already come through the storm. But if hell can convince your mind that you're still in a storm, you will never enjoy the present victory. You will never enjoy the new mercy. You will never enjoy the presence of God. In his presence, there is fullness of joy. Weeping endures for a night. It endured for a single night. That means that weeping has a time limit. There is an expiration date to weeping. But joy cometh in the morning. Cometh means continually. There is no expiration date for joy. We seem to put our expiration dates on good rather than bad things. We put our expiration dates on joy, but not weeping. Joy is going to come continually, but hell wants to torment your mind. It is time to let go of the wars of yesterday.

Many of their own Japanese troops tried to come and bring these men to safety, but they did not recognize their own. They did not recognize who their friends were. They thought they were being deceived. Their uniforms had long changed. They were so stuck in the past. Their thoughts and experiences were outdated. Have you ever been through something so hurtful that you don't even recognize who your friends are anymore? You get nervous when somebody says that they love you. When someone tells you that they love you, you tense up. You tense up because you are still nursing the wounds in your back that you suffered from being backstabbed. It is tough to heal alone and in isolation. You get nervous when someone says that they believe in you. You wonder what you are trying to get out of me? What is the angle? You are trying to take advantage of me.

You only think like that because your mind is still in warfare mode. You are stuck in survival mode. Your relationships are shallow because you will not let anyone get close to you again. You expect disappointment now. You are surprised when someone is faithful and loyal. You feel it is only a matter of time before they turn on you. You are stuck in a warzone in your mind. God is trying to transition you to a new height. But the trauma of yesterday is overtaking your viewpoint of today. God's trying to take you to a new level. These Japanese soldiers were so invested that they did not realize the battle was over. They had shed so much blood for a cause. They refused to accept that it was over. They had invested so many hours into that thing that they could not let it go. You have been free from that household for years, but your mind is at war. You have been free from that abusive relationship for years, but the mind is still at war. You've got to learn how to cast down the imaginations. You've got to learn to cast down the fear. You're not in survival anymore. You're not barely surviving anymore. This is your time to possess the land. This is your time to be more than a conqueror. This is your time to be the head and not the tail. This is your time to be above and not beneath. This is your time to take hold of what God has promised. No more rehearsing what happened yesterday. It is time to move forward.

In Madagascar, they have a very strange ritual. The ritual is called Famadihana. A particular tribe in Madagascar is intentional about ritual which involves visiting their ancestor's graves. They do not only visit these graves, but they actually open these graves. They take the bones from these graves and wrap them in new clothes. They call the ritual Famadihana, which also means "the turning of the bones." They take the bones up, put it on their shoulder, and celebrate. They start dancing with those bones from their ancestors' graves from hundreds of years ago. In this culture, they spend more on their graves than their houses. They brag about the new grave, not the new home they bought. They are more invested in their death than they are invested in their life. Their whole life, they are preparing to die. They dance with their ancestor's bones. They are more invested in their history than their future. One day, while dancing with the bones, they realized that many people in their area were getting sick and dying. There was a massive breakout of the bubonic plague, also known as the Black Death. The Black Death hadn't been seen for over 500 years since it took out one-third of Europe's population. After 500 years of this plague being absent, it arrived recently in Madagascar.

Researchers and scientists began to study to find the origin of the plague. Finally, after much research and effort, they discovered why the plague broke out. It happened whenever they started digging up their ancestor's bones. Whenever they began digging up their history. While digging up their history they made contact with the bubonic plague. The plague spread throughout the area and it destroyed many families. Where did it start? Whenever someone was more invested in digging up the past than digging toward their future. When you are so invested in what happened yesterday, it will try to sabotage and plague you today. You think it is innocent to keep revisiting the past, but those memories can plague you and your body today. It is time to move on. You have been dancing with the bones of the past long enough. There is nothing fun about it. It is time to bury the bones and walk into your future. Some of those graves were more expensive than houses. Bury the past and build your future. It is a challenge to let go, but you have to let it go for the next generation.

When you invest so much, it is tough to let go. When you invest so much into a cause. It is difficult to move on after investing so much time and energy into it. You invested so much time that it feels like you wasted time if it doesn't work out. You rehearse the past over and over in your head, trying to relive it. You are still trying to wrap your mind around the pain that was inflicted upon your soul. You are still in denial. Have you ever been through such trauma that it's tough to believe it even happened? Years later, you are still trying to process it. While processing it and denying it. Then, accepting it and denying it. Finally, God interrupts your thinking and says, "How long will you mourn over that?"

The longer you hold on to the past, the longer you delay grabbing the promise. Samuel had to battle with this because he was the prophet of Israel. He was the only man in the Old Testament who served as a judge, a prophet, and a priest. Samuel was not qualified to be a priest. He wasn't a Levite, but his walk with God was so powerful that God put him into the priesthood. God doesn't worry about your background. He doesn't worry if you have a great genealogy or not. He just sees your hunger. Your hunger supersedes your history. When God gets in the middle of your life, nothing else matters.

Samuel's life served as a transition point in Israelite history because he was the one who would usher in the prominence of the prophets and pave the way for them to have a relevant place in history. The people wanted a king; God told Samuel to make them a king. Samuel immediately began to pour himself into Saul. Samuel allowed Saul to sit with him in the high places. He began to treat Saul very kindly.

Samuel didn't want this, but he respected what the people wanted. He began to make an immediate investment in Saul's life. He spent time with him. He gave him the best of the food. He began to prophesy him to him over the things that would come. He filled his flask with oil and anointed him king over Israel. Saul would seek counsel from Samuel. A bond began to develop between Saul and Samuel. There came a time when Saul began to disobey the commandments of God; it truly grieved Samuel. God told Samuel that the kingdom would be taken away from him. Samuel began to weep over Saul. This was a broken dream. He was trying to make this thing work. He was trying to make this thing successful. He was trying to put all his strength and energy into making something work, but it didn't work. Samuel invested so much into Saul. God told Samuel, "I have rejected Saul."

God asked him, "How long will you mourn over Saul, seeing I've rejected him from reigning over Israel?" He says, "Listen, how long are you going to mourn over that broken dream?" How long are you going to mourn over your disappointment? Because the longer you mourn over it, the more energy you take away from your destiny. If it's gone, it means it's not a part of the plan. I know that's tough to accept. If it's gone, it means it's not a part of your future journey. This means this chapter has closed, but it doesn't mean the book has closed.

Whatever dream, failure, whatever you've been through and invested all of your life in, and it failed and you fell flat on your face, it just means the chapter has closed. It means the page has turned, but it doesn't mean your book is closed. God told him that it was time to fill his horn with oil. It's time to get you some fresh oil because yesterday's oil will not get you where God wants you to go. It's time to get a fresh wave of oil for where you are headed and where you are going.

This is that oil that's going to take you the rest of the way. This is that oil that's going to help you survive the broken dream and the broken season. This is that oil that's going to take you to a new height. This is that oil where you won't be remembered for what happened over Saul's life. You're going to be remembered for what you're anointing next. David is going to be greater than Saul. What is ahead of you will be greater than what is behind you.

How long will you mourn over Saul? How long will you mourn over that broken dream and that disappointment? How long will you mourn over that investment? Oh, I know it's terrible. I know it hurts. You invested so much because you thought you would be in that situation forever. I know you invested so much because you had a 30-year plan. You had a 10-year plan. But you never thought that there would be relationships that would be fractured. You never thought that there would be friendships that would be forever fractured. You never thought you would be abused or betrayed by someone you loved. You calculated them as a part of your journey, but they decided to leave the journey. They decided to go off course.

Stop mourning over everything you lost; remember you have some oil left. You didn't use all your oil on Saul. There's a little bit of anointing for David left, and there's a little bit of anointing for the future.

I know that there's a fear there. He said, "How long will you mourn over Saul, seeing I've rejected him from reigning over Israel? Fill thine horn with oil and go because I provided a king among Jesse's sons." Get your oil and go. Get the fresh oil. You couldn't see a future beyond your past experience. And because of that disappointment, you've been in no man's land. You have no energy to go forward, but you know you can't go backward.

I am writing to people stuck in the paralysis of pain. You can't give any energy forward, but you know you can't go backward. Put some oil in your horn again and get your feet moving. Because God has already provided a king among Jesse's sons. Fill your horn with oil because God has already prepared your future.

The only thing the future is waiting for is for you to move again. That's it. It's already done. It's already provided. You need to redirect your attention from what you lost. It is time to focus on the oil that you have left. We cry over our past but do not weep over our promise.

We must redirect our emotions. The emotional investment that we made in the past must be placed into the future. The zeal that we invested in yesterday must be put into today. How long will you brood over what they did to you? How long will you speak about the harm that they have caused? They are draining you. The painful memories are draining you. Every hero in the Old Testament had to deal with this type of transition. Instead of spending their energy managing the past, they had to start putting that energy into the promise. The Father of the Faithful is a great example of being in this war. He had to deal with his past (Ishmael) and the promise (Isaac).

Abraham left Mesopotamia for a promise from God that he would become a father of many nations. His wife was barren, and they were not able to have children. Trying to force God's hand, they made a mistake. Abraham slept with Hagar and had a child named Ishmael. For 13 years, he believed Ishmael was the promised son, but God told him the son would come through Sarah, not Hagar. God wanted to be glorified through Sarah's barrenness, not Hagar's youth. After almost 25 years of following God, Sarah finally had the promised son. Later God would speak to Abraham to sacrifice his promised son, Isaac. This was a test to see if Abraham loved the blessing more than the blesser. God tempted Abraham, but he didn't tempt him with sin. He tempted him with opportunity.

Genesis 22 is a pivotal point in the story of Abraham, but noticeably, no emotion of Abraham is mentioned. He cried over Sarah in Genesis 23:2. He weeps over her and is filled with fear while dealing with Pharaoh and Abimelech. But when it comes to his promise, he's numb. When it comes to his promise, there is no sign of any emotional investment. It is a notable absence. God told him to sacrifice his promise, and Abraham did not even shed a tear. God was going to take what was most valuable to him. God would take what he loved, yet no tears ran down Abraham's face. Instead, Abraham rose up early to complete the task. He immediately started the journey to sacrifice his son. Rising up early in the morning speaks to his obedience, but it also speaks subtly to something more profound. If

God asked any of us to give up something precious, we may obey but it will be grievous to us. It is not normal to not feel anything. It is a notable absence of emotion. Contrast this experience with how he reacted when he had to send Ishmael away.

Sarah saw the son of Hagar, the Egyptian she had born unto Abraham, mocking. Wherefore, she said, unto Abraham, "Cast out this bond woman and her son, for the son of this bond woman shall not be here with my son, even with Isaac." And the thing was very grievous in Abraham's sight because of his son. And God said unto Abraham, let it not be grievous in thy sight because of the lad because of thy bond woman and all that Sarah had said unto thee, hearken unto your voice to her voice. For in Isaac shall thine seed be called. The Bible says that whenever he had to detach from his mistake, the Bible says that it was very grievous to him.

When he told him to detach from his past, there was a deep-seated emotion on the inside of him. It was grievous for him. The word grievous in Hebrew is Yara, meaning to tremble or shake. Grievous means to convulse. Why is Abraham convulsing and trembling? He is so attached to his mistakes and past that he does not want to put them away. The issue with Abraham was that he was too emotionally invested in his mistake. He didn't have any energy or emotion to give to his promise. He was so invested in what had happened that he didn't have any more emotions to give to the possibility of losing his promise. He put so much energy into the past that he couldn't hold it together whenever he thought of losing Ishmael.

It was grievous. He was weeping. He was having a breakdown. Why? Because he believed that he deserved Ishmael. He thought that he deserved his mistake. To take away his mistake was to take away his identity. To move on from the past felt like a death sentence. Abraham felt that he and Ishmael would be inextricably connected forever. Getting rid of the mistake, he wept. Getting rid of the past, he convulsed. But there was no emotion whenever God told him to give up his promise. Why? Because he felt he didn't deserve it. He felt he didn't deserve the promise. There were no emotions when God asked to give it back. He thought to himself, "I knew this wasn't going to last. I knew it was too good to be true." We are scared to get emotionally invested in promises from God because we fear disappointment. We are afraid to put all our emotions into the future and the promise. We are scared to become one with the promise when we have been one with the mistake for so long. We fear the unknown future, so we cleave to the familiar past.

Grievous means "to be broken up and broken up internally." He couldn't even bear to do it. He couldn't bear to see his son walk away into the deserts of Beersheba. He didn't know if his son would live anymore. He was afraid of his mistake of dying. He was so invested in the past that he had no energy to give to his future.

He had invested so much in yesterday that he had no emotion for today. Abraham felt like he deserved his mistake. He wanted to do anything he could to hold onto it. He tried to hold on to the past and the failure. But when he came to the promise, he just gave it up freely without a tear or complaint. He rose early in the morning to give away the promise (Genesis 22). But he was full of emotion in Genesis 21. God has given you promises, but you let it go at the first sign of resistance. You freely let it go. Because you didn't feel like you deserved it in the first place.

But when it comes to your past, pain, trauma, or offense, it is grievous for you to let it go. I got my identity back there. Let it go. Move on. Walk in the future. You got an Isaac that you're carrying.

If I were to ask you, what did your past look like? You would be so vivid. You would take me back to the night. You would take me back to the day. You would take me back to the moment. You would tell me all the colors and what you were wearing. You would tell me everything that happened. You would be so vivid as you described the past. You would tell me about the ground that you walked on. You would tell me about the type of car that you had. You would quote verbatim what they said to you and what they said about your family. You are so specific when it comes to Ishmael. But you get very general if I ask about the promise and the future. If I ask you about the future, everything is hazy and gray. You say things like, "God's got it."

Be more specific. Tell me about where you and your family are headed. We give up on the possibility of a promise and rise up early to give it up. But if I were to say, Hey, now let go of that thing from the past. Let go of that thing from yesterday. Then you would say, "Let me tell you what happened on March 22nd, 1964. Let me tell you what happened on January 15th, 2002. Let me tell you what happened on February 3rd, 1994. Let me tell you what happened." But the question is, what about next year? Where are you going to be? What about five years from now? Where are you and your family going to be?

The first thing you do is say, "Hold on. Let me go back and reach for Ishmael. Because I have no emotion for the future. I'm reserving my emotions for the past. I have no emotion for the good in my life because I spend it on everything bad. I have no emotion for what's good about me. I'm reserving all my emotion for what's bad about me." Whenever someone gives you a compliment, you just nod your head. You do something good, and they say something good, but you forget about it quickly. But if anybody ever says something negative about you, you will think about it for months. You will think about it for years because you believe you deserve Ishmael and could never deserve Isaac.

You will stay up until midnight, grieving about the past and negativity. Why? It's tough to let go of your mistake, but it's easy to relinquish your promise.

Out of all the blessings that God gives you, you'll still refuse to let go of the mistake. Yes, you may carry Isaac, but you still hold Ishmael's hand. You have the past in one hand and the promise in the other hand. You are more willing to give away the promise than you are to give away your mistake. You will let somebody hold your promise for you. You are eager to give that baby away. But you never let anybody carry Ishmael. Not even God.

You come in and you let everybody hold baby Isaac. Because you don't feel like you deserve him anyway. But Ishmael, no. I got an emotional attachment to my pain. I can talk about pain all day. I can talk about my mistakes all day because I have defined myself by what happened with Ishmael. You have a death grip on Ishmael. And you're holding your promise with two fingers. Any time life starts tugging on the promise you say, "Okay, you can have it." But Ishmael, when God starts pulling on, letting go, Ishmael. You say, "Hey, God, listen, I won't talk to you anymore." It's too grievous because of how much investment I've made in Ishmael. The problem is that Abraham didn't express any emotion. It was a notable absence. In Genesis 21, he cries over the mistake. In Genesis 23, he cries over his loss of his wife. But yet, in the middle of Genesis 21 and 23 is 22, there's no emotion. Because we believe we deserve the mistake but don't deserve the promise.

When we are more emotionally invested in yesterday than we are today, our toxicity runs from healthy connections.

You have to get emotionally invested in your future. Do you ever notice that you have time for negativity all day? You can receive 10 calls of negative stuff, and your emotions will get involved. But if you get one call of positive things, you get stressed out. Isn't it amazing how our spirits are more attuned to Ishmael than Isaac?

People start aggravating you when they speak hope to you all the time. But we don't get stressed out with a lot of wrong information. Why? Because something in our subconscious expects bad. Because we believe we deserve that. But when it comes to the future, we want to doubt. If we get a call saying, "Hey, I got some money for you." The first thing you think is a scam. But when you get a call saying, "Hey, you owe money." The first thing you think is, "You are right, how much do I owe?"

But it matters where we invest our emotions.

We don't want to invest our emotions into Isaac or the promise because subconsciously, we believe it won't last long. In times past, good things didn't last long. You will not put your whole self into anything you think will not last.

It's like meeting a new person you don't think you will see for the rest of your life. You are not going to spend time talking about your family. You will not ask them how old they are or where they come from. You are not interested in their favorite color or occupation. You are uninterested because you don't expect to see them again. That's what we do with our promise. We have short conversations with the promise. With the promise, we are acquaintances. With the mistake, we are family members. It's time to be acquainted with your past, but make your future your family.

Do you believe more in the past than you do in the future? Do you believe more in your history and your mistakes than you do the promise?

Whatever you gave Ishmael, you better give it to Isaac. If you cried all night over Ishmael, it's time to have tears of joy over Isaac. If you stayed up all night because of Ishmael, it's time for you to stay up all night because of the glory of the promise coming before you.

Then he said to the king of Israel, "Draw the bow," and he drew it. And Elisha laid his hands on the king's hands. And he said, "Open the window eastward," and he opened it. Then Elisha said, "Shoot," and he shot. And he said, "The Lord's arrow of victory, the arrow of victory over Syria! For you shall fight the Syrians in Aphek until you have made an end of them." And he said, "Take the arrows," and he took them. And he said to the king of Israel, "Strike the ground with them." And he struck three times and stopped. Then the man of God was angry with him and said, "You should have struck five or six times; then you would have struck down Syria until you had made an end of it, but now you will strike down Syria only three times." So Elisha died, and they buried him (2 Kings 13:16-20).

This king had an incredible opportunity to defeat his enemies and go forward. The issue with this opportunity is that his kingdom was under the oppression of Syria for many years. It was tough for him to even consider him having dominion over the thing that was pushing him down.

When you are in something for a while, it can become normalized and familiar. Even though you know it's terrible. Can it be normalized and familiar? If you've been raised in a household that is really dysfunctional. Filled with abuse and toxicity. If you are raised in that, then that atmosphere is your normal.

As a result of the dysfunction, whenever you encounter people who really love you, it is bizarre. When you are raised in a dysfunctional environment and then you move out of that environment, it is difficult to keep long relationships or friendships. Because when people really embrace you and love you for who you are, you cannot handle it. You ask, "What's your motive?" Especially if your home was a performance-driven household. Dad didn't show love to you unless you performed perfectly. Mom didn't show love to you unless you crossed your T's and dotted your i's. It is challenging to grasp being loved just for being you.

Whoever said you had to do anything to receive love? Who taught you that? Every child that is born is supposed to be met with love by the mom and the dad. The child didn't do anything, but the parents did everything. Changing diapers. But you love that child. That child hasn't said, "I love you." It hasn't done anything. The child has only kept you up at night. That's about it. Your love for that child is not predicated on their ability or disability. It is not predicated on their performance. You love them because they are who they are.

For 30 years, Jesus did not accomplish anything significant. He did not open a blind eye, unstop a deaf ear, or heal anyone. Yet the first words from heaven after he was baptized were, "This is my beloved son, in whom I am well pleased." God's pleasure in you is not determined by your performance for him but by your relationship with Him. You are His child. You do not have to perform for God's love. You are his child. You are his beloved. The fact that you are here means that you are loved.

When you are raised in environments that are dysfunctional, it is customary to be run over. Your feelings are not considered. To earn "love," you must endure abuse. If you think about defending yourself, you feel guilty.

Anytime you think of believing in yourself, you feel prideful. When you're so used to being downtrodden, it is illegal and abnormal to believe in yourself. Over time, you develop a relationship with oppression. Now, you have no idea how to live life without being abused. You seek abusive relationships, friendships, companies, and churches that will misuse you because that is familiar. You feel naked and ashamed when you have free will. You run to anyone who will control you and your thoughts. When you leave an oppressive environment, you are scared that you are going to fail. They told you that if you are not under their control, you will die or something tragic will happen to you. Several years ago, I witnessed a leader complaining about someone leaving his church after she got married. She got pregnant and then suffered a tragic miscarriage. The leader rejoiced and said, "That is what she gets for leaving our church." He felt that God vindicated him through the miscarriage. Sickening. Oppressive leaders prophesy death when someone attempts to leave. This is why people stay in familiar abusive environments. They are fearful of the curses and retribution that will come. Be delivered from those curses.

Fight the war between trauma and transition. It is worth the fight. You have to move on and overcome this oppression. God gave you free will. You can make a decision. Oppression makes you feel that you are in rebellion for exercising free will. Make a choice. Choose transition over trauma.

This king was under oppression by the Syrians. This was his routine oppression and exploitation. The idea of him being free was a foreign concept. Have you ever been in something so long that you just accepted that's how it will be? You don't even fight it anymore. You don't even pray about it anymore. You don't even try to take dominion over it. You try to work around it because being free from that abuse is not a reality in your mind. You have to put these blinders on, right? You pretend that nothing's happening. Because if you address it, you're going to get agitated. If you focus on it, you'll get agitated because it's not aligned with where you want to go or what you want to be. But you don't dare to just take dominion over it.

This king was not only dealing with the oppression of Syria, but now he had to deal with the real possibility of the prophet dying. That is a traumatic experience. The prophet that he looked up to as a father is about to die. The prophet is on his deathbed. The king is going through the stages of grief. The memories flood his mind. He is overwhelmed at this moment.

The prophet says, "I have one more miracle before I die. Here's what I want you to do. I want you to take a bow and arrow. I want you to shoot out of a window, and you'll see that these arrows are the Lord's deliverance." The king is currently processing these words through the ears of trauma. The prophet is dying. While the trauma is happening, he is being presented with an opportunity. The more that the prophet talks, the more he is losing his life. The king is dealing with trauma and opportunity at the same time. The prophet tells him to shoot the arrow. This king is still processing the death that is occurring before his eyes. This king is literally with the prophet for his last hours. He shoots the arrows in the ground only three times. The prophet was angry. He said, "You should have shot it five or six times because then you would've beat the Syrians so bad that you would have consumed them. But you did it three times, meaning you will only win three times. You didn't beat him enough to take dominion over them."

You have got to keep attacking until you have dominion. You have to stay on the offense.

Why did the king put forth such minimal effort? It was not enough to defeat the enemy. He was in the war between trauma and transition. God is trying to transition you to a new level and a new way of thought. You've given all of your energy trying to manage the trauma of yesterday. You do not have any energy to give to your today or to your future.

Anytime you feel like doing something for God, you only give three arrows of effort. Why? Because you're spending all of your energy trying to manage what happened in your past, God said, "It's time to let go of what happened yesterday, and it's time to get an arrow in your hand again." You need to launch that thing until something begins to break and turn around in your life.

It is the war between trauma and transition because God is presenting you with an opportunity to go forward. He wants you to have victory and dominion. However, you are emotionally exhausted because you're still dealing with the trauma of what your dad did. You are still dealing with the trauma of what your mama did. You're still dealing with the trauma of what happened to you at the last company and your last church. All of your energy is wrapped up in trying to think about what happened, what you've been through, how they were wrong, and what they did was wrong. God is giving you an opportunity to go forward. But you are giving God three arrows of effort. That's not enough for you to get where you need to get. It's time to empty the quiver and let all the arrows out until something breaks. Launch all of the arrows into your future. Stop being timid. Come out of that fear.

You are giving three arrows worth of effort because you are still processing a death that occurred in your family. You are still processing the heartache that you have been through in your life. You may have been under oppression for years. You may think you don't have enough faith. I'm writing to you with tears; please keep shooting arrows. Empty the quiver. You gave your "best" years to the past. I'm asking you to give your "all" to the future. No need to hold back anymore.

I want you to keep on shooting until something begins to change and something begins to break. I don't want you to stop until you know your enemy will be consumed. I want you to empty the quiver. I know it's uncomfortable. I know you're a king and don't know what it feels like to pick up a bow and arrow, but it's not about feeling comfortable. It's about stepping out of your comfort zone. Stay on the offense.

It's not about the know-how. It's about your determination. Are you willing to do what it takes? Make up your mind, "I'm just going to keep firing. I'm just going to keep on firing." I'm going to keep on shooting until the prophet stops breathing. I still have power on the inside of me, and I'm not defined by the trauma. I'm defined by the transition. I'm going somewhere. I'm about to do something."

Keep on shooting. You are not just shooting for you. You are shooting for your family. You are shooting so that your son never has to deal with the Syrians ever again. You are shooting for your spouse and your grandkids. You are shooting for everybody that's coming behind you. You are shooting for your descendants. They never have to know what being under oppression felt like. Dad is fighting this battle for you. They never have to know what it feels like to be raped or to be a victim of domestic violence. You aren't just shooting for you. You are shooting for the generations coming behind you. You are defined by the transition.

I'm about to shout until hell trembles. I'm going to empty the quiver. I feel somebody's getting their zeal back. I feel somebody's getting their joy back. I feel somebody's getting their passion back.

I'm not just giving God a little bit anymore. I'm about to empty the quiver. I'm about to give him everything. I'm not going to do church, half-hearted. I'm not going to do church by just 25%. I'm about to go above and beyond. I'm about to empty the quiver.

Three arrows aren't enough to defeat your enemy. It's time to keep on shooting until something breaks in your family. It's time to keep on shooting until the bondage is destroyed. It's time to keep on shooting.

You need your energy for where you're going and for your transition. It's time to let go of what happened, pick up a bow and arrow, and launch into your future.

The whole nation was waiting on the king at that moment. He needed more than three arrows. He needed five or six. But if it was up to me, I wasn't giving God just five or six arrows. I'm giving God twenty. I'm giving God thirty because I'm going to make sure the devil never raises his head against my family again.

You're in the transition right now. This is the war. I know that you don't have energy. You've been dealing with opposition and resistance all week. I know you don't have energy, but this is war. I know you've been battling with family and fears. But this is the transition right here. This is the war. You've got to learn to forget those things which are behind and reach forth unto those things which are before. You've got to learn to just press forward. The more I think about the trauma, the more I feel stuck. It's sacrificing mental energy that's supposed to be put into your next book. You are spending the energy that is supposed to be put into your next business. You need that energy for your transition. You need to put that energy into your next level.

The disciples were fishing all night, and they caught nothing. Jesus arrives, saying, "I want you to launch out into the deep." Don't you understand Jesus? They caught nothing. Don't you know, they are still dealing with the trauma of being a qualified fisherman and still coming up barren. With all of their experience, they still caught nothing. They were still dealing with the trauma of being a failure. You are still dealing with the trauma of the mistakes that you committed in your life. But in this moment of trauma, you are telling me to launch out into the deep? You have to choose. Are you going to let the trauma define you, or are you going to let the transition define you?

The scary thing about transition is that you are going to a place you have never been. The frightening thing about trauma is that trauma is comfortable. The scary thing about trauma is you know your trauma. You can take me to the spot where you were taken advantage of. You could take me to the spot where they sabotaged you. You could take me to the spot that they didn't believe in you. You are comfortable with trauma. You are comfortable with the narrative. We can become comfortable with the statistics. But God says, "Hold on, put an arrow in your hand. I got a transition for you."

I know you've never seen it before, but there's victory coming for you that you've never seen before. You are going to conquer the thing that has tried to conquer you.

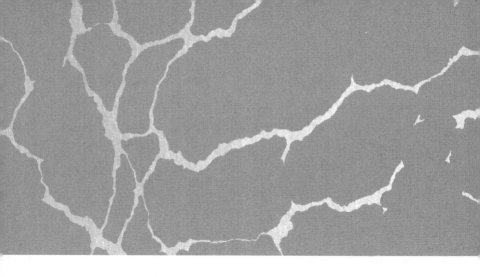

The same events that cause people to leave God are the same events that cause people to cleave to God. Trauma, offense, or abuse can make you leave or cleave; it just depends on who or what you are devoted to.

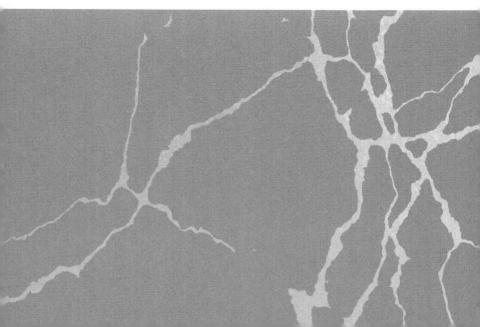

3

PRISONERS OF OFFENSE

*And there were four leprous men at the entering in of the gate:
and they said one to another, Why sit we here until we die?*

2 KINGS 7:3 KJV

I t was in the early 14th century that there was a duke by the name of Reginald III. As a duke in Belgium, he was in the middle of a war with his younger brother Edward. They fought for years because Edward wanted to usurp Reginald III. Edward was willing to fight Reginald for as long as possible; he was desperate for his brother's throne. After many years of struggle, Edward finally overthrew his brother and took the throne from him. He imprisoned his brother in a castle. The unique aspect of this imprisonment was that he left the door unlocked and open. Reginald III could walk out of the prison whenever he wanted to. He was imprisoned, but he was not confined in any way. He had no handcuffs or locks on his body that prevented him from leaving. He could not leave the room because Edward knew his older brother's weakness. Reginald's one weakness was food. He was a foodie before there were foodies. He loved desserts, and as a result, historians described him as a huge man. Edward knew that he needed to hold Reginald captive, so all he needed to do was continue feeding him some delicious food. Reginald became so large from eating these delicacies that his body could not fit through the open door.

It is rumored that Edward remarked, "I never imprisoned my brother. I just gave him more of what he wanted." He knew Reginald's appetite.

He had become a prisoner of his own appetite. Reginald sat there for a decade and ate everything on his plate. Something within him so desperately wanted to escape. Still, he would not and could not stop eating what his enemy was serving him. It was wrong what Edward did to his older brother. This was an offensive act. But it is so easy to focus on the external events that happened to Reginald. Reginald could spend all day speaking of the offense that his brother committed against him. The only issue is that he is still in prison. Mulling over the events could not deliver him; he needed to stop eating what his enemy was feeding him. Stop eating what the enemy is feeding you. Hell wants you to sit down in the offense and continue feeding you more offenses so that you never get out of prison. Stop eating the devil's cake (Not the literal cake, but metaphorically). Stop eating what he is putting on your plate. He will continue feeding you offenses to keep you from focusing on your freedom. He will continue feeding you so you are focused on everything that has been done to you instead of focusing on what it takes to come out of prison.

The enemy watches how we handle bad things that happen to us. The enemy watches our response level. The devil watches to see if we get paralyzed from progression after we get hurt. He will do anything to keep you from moving forward. He will keep on feeding us that same offense to keep us stagnant. He desperately wants to keep you in place because he fears what you will become. More than anything, he wants you to continue rehearsing what everybody has done to you. But you must recognize the power that you have within you. You have the power to get up and get out of that prison. You will come out of the prison better than you went in. Put your trust in God. Whatever hell tries to destroy you, God will use it to develop you. We will win this war.

Your enemy watches how you handle the offense. The devil is worse than the "happiness police" because he is not a vulture; he is a serpent. You can see a vulture coming from a mile away, but a snake will sneak up on you. Your enemy will use other people to continue feeding you offenses. He hopes that it will paralyze you in your mission. The enemy wants to paralyze you from making any progress. He will do anything to prevent you from moving forward. He watches how our faces react to the bitter taste of offense. If we continue eating and savoring the taste, he will continue giving it to us. He wants you to eat offense until you get so large that you cannot fit through the doors of freedom God has opened for you. It's time to clean the plate today and decide that you are not living in offense anymore. You will come out of this prison better. You are coming out of this prison with abundance. You are coming out of this prison with a future.

When bad things happen, hell watches how we handle it. The best way to handle something terrible is to go straight to the Lord. But if you are dealing with abuse, assault, or anything like that. Then, you need to go to the Lord and not be afraid to call law enforcement. There must be eternal and personal accountability.

We are often paralyzed in the offense because we continue rehearsing what happened to us. He will feed you offenses to get your focus off of God and your purpose. He will try to shift your attention to the person that hurt you. You went through a divorce; you were traumatized by that. McDonald's gets your order wrong the day after your divorce is finalized. Now, you are offended at McDonald's. You commit to never going to McDonald's again. You head to Burger King the next day. Your whopper wasn't fresh; you are offended by Burger King. You commit to never eating at Burger King again. The next day, you confide in a friend and find out that friend is telling people about your business. Then you commit to not having friends anymore. Now, you are starting to get large off of the offenses. The offenses start piling up. Now, you justify not moving forward in your purpose. A door is open for you; you must bring the pain to God. Too many people depend on you to become what God has called you to become. We need you to come out of that prison. You are too gifted to stay in that prison of offense. You are too important to the world and the kingdom of God. Come out of that offense. Bring the pain to God. You have an open door set before you. But we justify ourselves. We feel like we are getting revenge on them by holding on to the offense. 30 years have passed. 10 years have passed. 5 years have passed. 6 months have passed since the offense happened. You are holding on to the pain because somehow, in your subconscious, you believe that you are hurting them by not moving on and letting it go. The people that hurt you have moved on. They are raising their families. They are going on vacation. While you are still in prison. You tell yourself, "I'm not coming out of this prison until they apologize." Well, that means that they still have power over you. Most people will never apologize to you. Welcome to humanity. Unfair. Yes. Wrong. Yes. Welcome to humanity. If you do not move on, you hurt your kids. Now, your children are raised in your prison. Now, they have a story of offense and abuse. Stop the cycle. Come out of the prison. Let your kids see the sun. They have only seen the "cell" version of you. Show them the "free" version. Show them how to overcome obstacles and fears. The Duke Reginald III was eating in a prison of offense while his younger brother Edwards had moved on. The offender is out there loving their new life while you are complaining about what they did to you 10 years ago. The people who hurt you have forgotten about you. They don't remember what they did to you; you are not the only one that they hurt. This happened 30 years ago. They have grandkids now. But you are still secretly following them on social media. You are looking at them smiling and holding them grandkids. You think to yourself, "Who do they think they are. After all that they did to me!" You remember their sinful actions down to the very second it happened. They hurt you 25 years 37 days 6 hours 5 minutes and 27 seconds ago. You squint your eyes while you see their success on social media. You try to scroll through and ignore it. But you keep scrolling through their profile. Every post they make, you are still waiting to see if they will ever address what they did. You read into their comments. They may not even remember your name. You scroll and scroll and scroll. Then you accidentally hit "like" one of their photos. After the embarrassment of doing that, you block their profile. You block them for three days, then you go back to unlock them and continue to obsession all over again. They are living the life; you are in the prison of offense. You are obsessing and getting bigger and bigger on these offenses. Satan will just keep on giving you offense. You must remember that Jesus holds the offender accountable. But in this day and age, no one talks about the offender. We know that no one should live offended. But we also know that no one should live as an offender either. People tell the offended to forgive, but no one tells the offender to stop abusing people. People tell the offended to get over it. Still, no one tells the offender to stop sexually assaulting and raping people. The offender and the offended must come to Jesus to be made whole. Each person has a personal responsibility to get into alignment with God. In that alignment, we will treat one another with the dignity we deserve because we are created in the image of God. The offender's healing is not your responsibility. Your healing is your responsibility. Get your eyes off of them; they cannot help you. Get your eyes on Jesus because God will heal you in front of the people who hurt you. Whenever an offense has been committed against you. A wrong act. An illegal act against you. But nothing happens to the person, we feel like we're putting judgment on them by sitting in our prison. We feel we are hurting them the more we rehearse the hurt. But we are only hurting ourselves. Our marriages. Our ministries. Our kids. When you hold on to offense, it taints your viewpoint of everything. Only seeing things through the lens of offense will lead to delusion. One reason that people hold on to offenses is because they have been fed a lie concerning forgiveness. People tell you that no matter how much someone abuses you, you cannot detach from them. They say that if you detach from them, you haven't forgiven them. This is a lie from the pit of hell! It is possible to forgive, but never allow them access to you again. Some people should be forgiven, but a rapist should not have constant access to your life. I feel that people are getting delivered while reading this. People try to shame you into forgiving people. Because of this tainted concept of forgiveness, you would rather embrace the bitterness of offense. Both of these concepts are traps that will enslave you. It is time for a biblical concept of forgiveness and reconciliation. Forgiveness only needs one person, but reconciliation needs both people. Reconciliation means that both people are willing to make concessions in order to restore their relationship. If only one side makes concessions, but the other side refuses to move or change their harmful/toxic/abusive behaviors, then reconciliation is not possible. Reconciliation is always the aim, but sometimes, we must settle for forgiveness with healthy boundaries. Whenever you forgive, that does not mean you have to continue to expose yourself to abuse and toxicity. Take a breath. Process the pain that they have caused. Grieve over that pain. After you have processed all the heartache that they have caused, forgive. But no one can force themselves back into your life. You decide who you allow in; you determine whether they are a safe relationship. Jesus Christ died for the sins of the world. He cried, "Forgive them, for they know not what they do." Jesus Christ did everything necessary to have a restored relationship with mankind. But we decide if we want to reconcile with him or not. Jesus Christ created the path for reconciliation, but we must align ourselves to be reconciled with him. Reconciliation takes both parties to come into alignment. If they are unwilling to repent of their sins and turn from their wicked ways, how can two walk together except that they agree? Forgive and move on; that is your responsibility. Because of the lies concerning forgiveness, many have taken an unhealthy alternative: seething in bitterness. Instead of moving forward with your life, you sit in the prison of offense.

When an offense has been committed against you, the devil wants you to do is to remain on defense. You are guarded all the time. You are defensive in your conversations and relationships. You cannot open up to your spouse because you are so defensive. You cannot handle jokes because you are defensive. You do not fellowship after church because you are defensive. Your relationships are shallow because you are defensive. The enemy wants you to stay on defense. In sports, they have something called offense. To overcome offense, you must learn to go on *offense*. Same word, different meaning. Same word, different context. Same word, different power. Instead of living on defense, it's time to live on the offense.

Vince Lombardi was a famous coach for the Green Bay Packers. They lost the championship the year before. In summer camp, the returning players had a meeting with the coach. They're still trying to overcome the pain of what happened to them. Their first meeting with Coach Lombardi in summer camp was one for the ages. He sat down these professional NFL players and said, "This is a football." He brought them back to the fundamentals. He was simply reminding them to not focus on the losses but to focus on the basics. Focus on the main thing, "This is a football." These NFL players had been playing football since they were toddlers, but they had to be reminded of the basics. Professionals do many of the same drills as middle schoolers and high schoolers. Professionals master the basics. Same drills, different mastery levels. But through the ups and downs of a sport, you never graduate from the basics. Coach Lombardi brought them back to the main thing. It's not about how many losses you had. It's not about what happened to you. It's not about what your mom or dad did to you. "This is a football," and the most important thing on the field is the football. It's the most important thing. It doesn't matter how good you play your position if you ignore the football. The enemy wants to get you so defensive that you forget about the main thing.

My college basketball coach taught me that the most important thing on the court is not a person. It's the basketball. You can have the best player in the world on your team, but it does not matter if they do not have basketball. They cannot be great without the basketball. The basketball is the most important object on the court. If people are more focused on a person than they are on the ball, then they lose. Stephen Curry. Tom Brady. Messi. They are great because of what they can do with the ball. The main thing is the ball, not the person. If someone hits an athlete in the chest during the game, they must stay focused on the main thing instead of attempting to get revenge on their opponent. If you forget about the most important thing on the court and try to get revenge on your opponent, you will miss the mission. The opponent will try to get in your head so that you forget about the ball and focus your attention on them. The more you focus on them, the more you direct your energy toward them instead of the main thing.

Basketball taught me a lot about focusing on what is most important. What is the main thing? What is the goal? Every team wants to play a home game because it is a more positive experience with more of your fans. In away games, it was customary to get cursed out. It is normal in sports for the crowd to get loud and yell profanities at the athletes. It is to distract them from the main thing. The fans hope that the players take it personally and forget about winning. While shooting free throws, the crowd will get deafening and distracting. They will hold up pictures of you and your family. They threaten to hurt you if you make the shot. When I traveled playing basketball, I would get cursed out all of the time. They would mock and jeer all the time. Every athlete has experienced this. Disciplined players know how to push past the offenses and get the mission accomplished. Every athlete that has ever played has had to face verbal abuse. They don't stop their lives or their purpose to ruminate over it. They understand that human nature can do harm, but they do not allow the offense to keep them from the main thing. We have heard things like, "he earned criticism." Criticism is not given; it is earned. The reward for greatness is criticism, contention, and conflict. Every professional must know how to manage it and use the negativity to push them into positivity. Anyone great has had to overcome some type of pain or abuse. Study all the greats in the history of the world. If the athlete allows these words to affect them, it will affect their productivity and purpose in their lives. They must practice for hours and perfect their craft so that they can handle the noise. Regardless of distractions or pain, they have disciplined themselves to keep the main thing in view. In practice, they would hit us with boxing bags while we shot and did layups. They were teaching us to expect adversity but still get the mission accomplished.

"This is a football." "This is a basketball." Well, this is a Bible. I know you lost things. I know you suffered. I know you've been through pain, but the Bible has to be the main thing and superior to your feelings, pain, emotions, abuse, offense, trauma, and losses. The Bible is still the most important thing. The enemy wants to distract you from the main thing. Everything is about the word of God. The enemy wants you to focus on those who hurt you instead of living by the eternal principles of the Bible. He wants you to focus on the offense instead of going on offense.

Instead of focusing on bearing fruit and taking the good news to the world, the enemy wants us to focus on those who hurt us. The enemy wants you focused on the abusers and offenders. He wants you to focus on their harmful actions instead of trying to conform to the image of Jesus Christ. He wants to use offenses as an excuse to justify our lack of obedience and transformation. But it is time to leave prison and go on the offense.

The main thing is the Bible. The main thing is Jesus Christ: the word made flesh. Today, you are no longer focusing on the offense. You are focusing on going forward: offense. You are not backing up on defense anymore. You are going forward on offense. You are not attacking people. You are attacking goals and dreams. You are attacking your purpose every morning. To overcome offense, you have to go on *offense*. You are attacking your next book. You are attacking your next business. You cannot hold on to the offense and remain on *offense*. You are focused on your relationship with God. The past is not sufficient motivation. The offense of the past cannot compare to your *offense* in the future. The evil that has been done to you cannot compare to the good that you are about to do.

The Bible says that this gospel should be preached in all the world. That's what you call offense. The Bible says that the gates of hell shall not prevail against the church. You know what that is? Offense. The church is on the offense, not the defense. We are not afraid of what the enemy can do to us; we have been equipped to make a difference in this world. When a church is no longer on offense, it gives room for the devil to make it a place for offenders and the offended. When we are about the Lord's business everything flows better. Walking in love and purity. Walking in godliness. It's time for you to go back on offense. You are going to make the devil wish that he never touched your kids. The enemy is going to wish that he never touched your marriage. You are going on the offense in prayer, forgiveness, love, compassion, grace, mercy, and zeal. You have been paralyzed while focusing on the progress of your enemies. It is time to focus on the progress of the word of God in your life. Take your eyes off of your enemy and appreciate what God is trying to do in your life.

A perfect example of moving forward is these four leprous men who had endured multiple offenses in their lives. They endured physical and emotional wounds. They were isolated from their community and bleeding as a result of their trauma. They had to learn how to walk with their wounds. Leprosy is a degenerating skin disease. They were missing limbs. All four of them could rehearse the hell that they had gone through. No matter how hard they tried, they could not forget about the things that had crippled them. They were cut off from everything meaningful. They could not ever see their wives again according to the Levitical laws. They could not say good night to their children. They were lepers, so they were cut off from their community. Lepers had to be outside the camp, announcing to everyone that they were unclean. These were men who were damaged by society. Wounded due to family issues. Neglected by the priests. The priests decided who was a leper or not. Wounded by family, cut off, and even neglected by the priests who were the religious authority. It was the religious authority of the priests that decided who was leper or not. The lepers could have spent their whole life getting bitter at the religious authority of the priests. They could have spent their whole life getting bitter at the religious leaders of their day. They were offended by what had happened to them. It seemed so unfair. But while they were wounded, they said, "Why sit here until we die?" They asked themselves, "Why stay here in this condition until we die? If I stay where I am, I'm going to die. If I go back to where I came from, I'm going to die. My only option is to make a decision and move forward." If lepers can decide to move forward, no matter what offense or hell you have been through. You can make a decision today move forward.

They made a decision to make some type of progress. They got sick of sitting there in their prison of offense. They were done thinking about what religious leaders had done and contemplating the years that they lost. They were done thinking through the divorce that happened. I don't know if they stayed married. All I know is that the wife had to dwell on the inside, and the lepers had to dwell on the outside. If there was any leprosy in his house, the scripture states that the house had to be destroyed. When the leprosy got into the walls, the first commandment in Leviticus was to destroy the whole house so that the leprosy didn't spread. How would you feel if you were not only diagnosed with leprosy and had a wound and an offense, but now the house that you built with your own hands is being torn down. You can't live there anymore, and neither can your kids. Your kids could be on the streets because of an unfortunate wound that happened. They rehearsed the offense in their mind, but finally, after spending time with one another, they decided it was time to get out of their pity party and make some progress. Why sit in this prison of offense until we die? They said, "If we stay where we are, we're going to die. If we go back to where we came from, we're going to die. But if we go forward, we shall live. They pretty much said, "Even if the future kills me, we're still going to die."

If I'm going to die, let me die going forward. If I'm going to fail, let me fail forward. You have to take a risk. You have to get tired of living in Egypt. You have to get tired of thinking about what Egypt did to you. You have to get tired of living in the wilderness.

Thank God for the manna in the wilderness. Thank God for the quail in the wilderness., but you have to get tired of living in the monotony of the day-to-day and thinking over what happened to you. It's time to go to the promised land. You have to get where the promise is. You have to get to where my destiny is. We have shouted over what you were delivered from. You were delivered from an abusive relationship. You were delivered from abusive parents. You were delivered from these things that happened to you. You were delivered from Egypt, but now you're sitting there in the wilderness and murmuring like the Israelites. You are complaining, and you are mad at God for all the hell that you went through. But it's not enough to be delivered from something. You've got to be delivered to something. You came out of it to go into it. You came out of hell, but you are about to experience heaven. You went out of the problem to get to the promise. You came out of the hurt to get to the healing. There's healing on the other side of this offense.

There is power on the other side of this heartache. Everyone loves talking about what they were delivered from. No one talks about what they are being delivered to. A package is not delivered until it leaves one destination and arrives at the next destination. You are not delivered until you get where God wants you to be. I'm glad you have a testimony, but I rejoice that you have a future. What is ahead of you is greater than what is behind you. He brought you out from the abuse to bring you into the anointing. The progress started when they stopped rehearsing the past and started looking to the future.

The progress started with their mentality.

That's where the progress started. You could still be in the prison cell, but as long as your mind is out of the prison cell. You are on your way out. Once your mind gets out of this, the body will follow the mind out.

You have to get your mind right. You may be in sin right now. You may be in hell right now. You may be on offense right now, but as you read this book, your mind is transformed. While in your sin. While in your struggle. While in your hell. The mind starts being transformed by the power of God. Even in prison, if you have a changed mind, you will not be in that prison much longer. You are coming out of this. That's how you get out of the prison of offense. You start getting into the word of God and into the presence of God. His presence will persuade your mind to come out of there.

These lepers decided to go in the right direction. They dragged their feet, most likely missing toes, limping, hurting, and moving slowly, but they were going forward. It does not matter how long it takes to get to the promise; as long as you are moving forward, that is the victory.

No matter what, they were walking towards their future—messed up and funny-looking. While they were limping forward, the Lord sent a noise into the enemy's camp. The noise was so loud that the enemy said, "There are kings coming after us."

When the enemy saw their commitment to progress, they didn't call them lepers. They called them kings. They didn't call them lepers. They called them royalty. Why? Because although offended, hurt, and wounded, they decided to go forward. Their mind came out of prison, and gradually, they pulled their body towards the future. They committed to making some sort of progress. They were moving forward while they were scared. While they were paranoid. The camp was empty. The lepers sat down and ate and drank. They grabbed the treasure and hid it. They hid it because they were expecting mischief to come upon them. While they were getting the victory, they were still scared.

While they were succeeding, they still had the fear of losing something or losing everything, but they kept going forward. This is true courage, moving forward in the face of fear. Every person reading this book right now has made some type of progress. I commend you. I honor you. While those lepers were messed up, wounded, and broken. They were crawling forward. They were inching forward. To come out of that prison, you must learn how to celebrate the progress that you have made.

Those lepers said one to another, "We do not well. This day is a day of good tidings, and we hold our peace. If we tear till the morning light, mischief will come upon us. Therefore, we may go and tell the king's household." They did not want to keep it to themselves. They not only wanted to celebrate their progress, but now they committed to going on the offensive. Now, it is time to testify. The enemy does not like it when you go on the offensive and start thanking God for your progress on your journey. If you want to know how to go on the offense, start thanking God for the progress that you've made. You're not perfect. You still have flaws. You still have things that you are battling through, but you are inching forward. I want to take time in this book to celebrate you. You have made incredible progress. I am proud of you. More importantly, God is proud of you.

You're not the same person you were three weeks ago. You're not the same person you were a month ago, ten years ago, five years ago. There has been progress. You are still battling issues and wounds, but there's been progress. Don't hold your peace. Thank God for progress. Now it's time to open your mouth and start testifying. It is time to go on the offensive. Hell tried to kill your family, but by the grace of God, you are still here. Hell wanted to destroy you, but by the grace of God, you are still here. You should not have a sound mind right now, but by the grace of God, you do. You were still showing up to work while recovering from domestic violence. You are a hero. You are a champion. You were still serving others and bringing your kids to school while you felt that your life was falling apart. You shouldn't be where you are today, but by the grace of God, you are. You were taking college courses while fighting depression, and you were still able to complete school. I honor you!

You have what it takes to go on the offensive because we overcome by the blood of the lamb and by the word of our testimony. Tell your story in a redemptive way. Tell your story from the future, not from the past. You went through the pain, but you possessed the promise. Go on the offensive. Celebrate the progress. I know you may still be in the same situation. I know you still may be healing, but I celebrate you because I see progress. Taking time to read this book is progress. You may even still be in prison, but I celebrate you because I can see your mind coming out. Once the mind is out of the prison, the body will follow. You're coming out of the prison. Reginald III wouldn't stop eating for 10 years. His brother, Edward, finally lost the

war, and afterward, they freed Reginald. When they freed him from
the room, he could not fit through the open door. They had to cut
out a massive hole in the wall for him to come out. He was finally
free and able to sit on his throne, but he died a few months later after
being free. His health took a massive hit because he was a prisoner
of his offenses. Even when there was a victory, his health wasn't in
the place to be grateful and appreciate the win. Stress is called "the
silent killer." It's been messing with your body. You've been having
migraines. Your joints have been swollen. You visit the doctor, and
they say nothing's wrong. You don't have illness, but your body is
in pain. Stress has been eating you alive. Stress has been feasting on
you. One of the great ways to eliminate stress is to have that gratitude. Start thanking God for life. This is your first step coming out
of the prison of offense. This is your first step out of the prison cell,
out of the hurt, out of the offense.

They did a study on how emotional pain affects the body. They had
people who had suffered rejection to start taking ibuprofen. After taking ibuprofen, they immediately felt better. The body treats emotional
wounds the same way it does physical wounds. Rejection, neglect, and
verbal abuse can take a physical toll on the body. After taking ibuprofen, they saw an improvement in their mood. Emotional wounds
feel like physical wounds. Spiritual and emotional wounds do affect
the body. Let this hurt do so that you can be free.

I'm not here to judge you for the things that you are still holding on
to. No, I'm celebrating you today because you've still committed to
making some progress despite it all. Still hurt, but making progress.
Still limping but making progress. Still crying, but making progress.
I know God's going to do something in you as long as you commit to
going forward. God's going to fight the battle for you. God's going to

restore your mind. God's going to heal your body. You need to thank the Lord for healing you from the inside out. You need to thank the Lord that you don't look like what you've been through. He's been your sustainer. He's been your provider. He's been your healer. He's been your strength. He's been your song. He's been that anchor for the soul. He's been that rock of ages. He's been your healer, and he will not throw you away. He will not put you away as damaged goods, but Jesus is rejoicing over you right now. The angels are rejoicing over you right now. The angels rejoice over one sinner who repents no matter how damaged the sinner is. When that sinner says, "I'm going in the right direction," all of heaven rejoices over that sinner.

You are going on the offense with your praise, your voice, your worship, and your gratitude. You will not be on defense anymore. You are confident going forward because God is working on your mind.

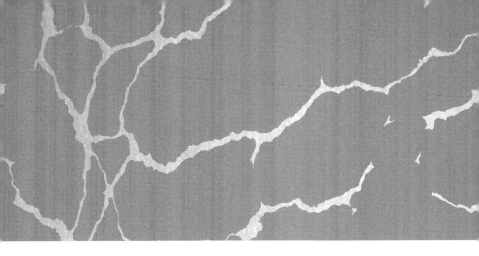

I believe in forgiveness with all my heart, but that does not mean repeatedly going back to entertain toxic relationships that are a threat to your mental health and well-being. Sometimes, you not only need to forgive but also...move on.

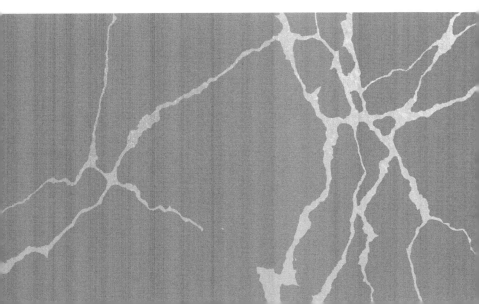

4

MIND OVER MANNA

And the Lord said unto Joshua..." God said, "The Lord said
unto Joshua, 'This day have I rolled away the reproach of Egypt
from off you.' Wherefore, the name of that place is called Gilgal
unto this day and the children of Israel encamped in Gilgal.
And kept the Passover on the fourteenth day of the month
and even in the plains of Jericho. And they did eat of the old
corn of the land on the morrow after the Passover, unleavened
cakes, and parched corn in the selfsame day. And the manna
ceased on the morrow after they had eaten of the old corn of
the land; neither had the children of Israel manna anymore:
but they did eat of the fruit of the land of Canaan that year.

JOSHUA 5:9-12 KJV

There is an English idiom, "mind over matter," which describes an impossible task before an individual, but through their mind, they are able to overcome it. This idiom describes underdogs and those who are not supposed to win. Those below the standard use their minds to overcome difficult obstacles. An example is a marathon runner who tears their hamstring in the middle of a race. The marathon runner's body will start shutting down because, physically, there is no way that they can finish the race. But somehow, through the strength of their mind, they are able to overcome their limitation and finish the race. The mind allowed them to overcome their physical limitation. The mind pushed their bodies to new heights that had never been achieved before. Their mind willed them to finish the race despite the injury and pain in their body.

The mind is so vital to the Christian life. God desires for you to be transformed by the renewing of your mind. It's not enough to do the right behaviors. Somehow, the right behaviors have to be fueled by the right mind. If you want to be changed, you have to allow God to come into your mind and start changing some things. God is trying to take his people to a new level, but many are hindered by old mentalities. Old mindsets hinder new miracles. Old memories can sabotage new moments. In order to be in a position to receive the promise, you must shed off the old way of thinking.

The children of Israel were in Egypt for 430 years. They were slaves for 430 years. They endured the whips of Egypt for generations. But in one day, God delivered them from the whips of Egypt. They walked through the wilderness, and God tried to bring them into the promise. However, they still had an Egyptian mindset of slavery, so they sabotaged the promise. They wandered in the wilderness for 40 years. Finally, they went into the Promised Land. When they entered the Promised Land, God's first words were these: "This day have I rolled away the reproach of Egypt from off of you."

Hold on one second. The children of Israel had been out of Egypt for 40 years, but God said, "This day have I rolled away the reproach of Egypt." The word reproach literally means "harsh words." It took them a day to get delivered from the whips of Egypt, but it took 40 years for them to get delivered from the words of Egypt. It wasn't just that they whipped them. It was what they said while they were whipping them. "You're grasshoppers. You're nothing. You're nobody." Whenever God tried to take them to another level, they could not believe they were worthy. Because they still heard the words of their past that were spoken over them. They were walking for 40 years free from Egypt, but they couldn't shake the words off of them. They saw themselves as grasshoppers because that is what they were told that they were while living in Egyptian bondage. They still saw themselves through the lens of their abuse, although they were free.

You have been delivered from that trauma for 50 years. You were set free from that offender for 20 years. You came out of that abusive household over 5 years ago. You got out of that domestic violence situation 30 years ago. You have long been delivered from the whips. But the problem is you are still carrying the words. You are afraid to be what God has created you to be. You are so scared to be great. You are afraid to move on because the words will not let you move on. You are afraid to be successful because your father always told you that you would be a failure, but you are still holding on to the words. You are so scared to move forward because you are still carrying those traumatic words in your spirit. You are no longer whipped in your body, but you are still being whipped in your mind. It is the mind that must be persuaded that there is safety. The mind must be convinced that the future is more significant. An animal caged for its entire life does not know what to do with freedom when released back into the wild. The mindset of the creature must adapt to open spaces. You were caged like an animal.

You paced back and forth in your cage. You are free to possess the promise now, but you are still pacing back and forth and roaming in circles because of your mind. The Israelites were walking in circles for 40 years. It's time to break the cycle. When they stepped into the promised land, they were in Gilgal, which means "circle." It was a full-circle moment. But this time, God addressed the source of the problem. He said, "Today, I am rolling the harsh words of Egypt from off of you." Now, you can go into your destiny. Now, you can grab ahold of your future. God rolled the harsh words off them and deposited his eternal words into them.

You may feel that the words spoken over you in childhood do not matter. It does matter. You were too young to process those types of wounds. The words try to follow you through life. Psychologists say that your inner voice that you have with you sounds a lot like your parent's voice. That is the voice you revert to to guide you in your decision-making. You need God's words to replace the harsh words. God is going to roll the harsh words away. While you are reading this book, the harsh words are disappearing. You are a child of God. You are chosen. You have a future. You were put on this earth for a purpose. You do matter. God is not finished with you. God loves you. He is proud of you. God is changing your mindset. It took one day for them to get delivered from the whips, but it took 40 years for them to get delivered from the words. Today, God is delivering you from the words.

If you want to be successful, you have to get a mindset for victory. You have to get the mindset of an overcomer. If you have the mentality of an overcomer, then nothing can take you down. No matter how insurmountable the obstacles may be. If your mind is in the right place, you will get through. If your mind sees itself as only a victim. No matter how much someone loves you, you will self-sabotage. If you have the mind of a victim, no matter how friendly people are to you. No matter how loving people are to you. Your mind will continue to sabotage those relationships. With a victim mentality, all of your relationships will be shallow. You may have been a victim, but you don't have to live the rest of your life as a victim. You were a victim for a moment, not a lifetime. A moment of abuse does not mean you have to be defined by the abuse for the rest of your life. It's time to conquer the narrative with your mind. You are not defined by what happened. We must allow the word of God to cleanse our minds so that we can have deep relationships.

The issue with abuse and trauma is that after you go through it, you become hypervigilant. You are watching people's facial expressions and how they tap their feet. You are constantly analyzing people because you are trying to figure out if they are safe. You have been married for

15 years and are still trying to determine if your partner is safe. You monitor their moods. They had a bad day at work, but you think it is your fault if they are sad or angry around you. Hypervigilance is a survival tactic. Hypervigilance is not spiritual discernment. People who have been through trauma think that they have the gift of spiritual discernment because of how well they analyze people's moods and habits. Hypervigilance is your body's way of protecting itself, it is not inherently spiritual. Your analysis can be completely off when everything is seen through this survival lens. Breathe. Allow God to heal your mind. Not everyone is trying to harm you or destroy you. Breathe. Don't allow these survival tactics to sabotage another relationship. Receive the mind of Christ.

Trauma and abuse can make you believe that you will die early. You may have dreams of dying young. If a survivor does not have a fear of death, then they have a fear of success. You treat success like it's a cliff. The brain is designed to keep you from danger. If you are afraid of success (the cliff) then the mind will not allow the body to get in alignment with successful behaviors. Your mind will not allow the body to manifest the right behaviors: You will not get the right behaviors until your mind stops being afraid.

People have a fear of success because they made success synonymous with pride. You want to be successful but are afraid to fall off pride, so you flee success. There is something in you that longs to be great, but you are scared that you will fall for pride. Humility is not a destination. Biblical humility actually leads you to elevation. Humble yourself under the mighty hand of God, and he shall exalt you. But what happens when God starts trying to exalt you? You begin to self-sabotage. You say, "No, I got to stay humble. I got to stay humble." No. Humility is not an abode; it's an attitude. Humility is not living in a specific place; it is living in purpose. You can have an attitude of humility with a billion dollars. You can have an attitude of humility with a million dollars. You don't have to be broke to be humble. You don't have to be small to be humble.

Humility is not a destination. It's an attitude you can have whether on the mountain or in the valley. If you are going through a storm or walking in peace. Humility, you can have it at all times. Some people are so scared of success or blessing that the only time they feel comfortable is in failure. They breathe out a sigh of relief when they fail. You have been through so much pain and failure that you are okay not walking in your purpose. The only time you are paranoid is when you walk in blessing. The blessing of God is too good so you find a way to self-sabotage. When you are in trouble, you are relaxed. Whenever you are being blessed, you are tense. This has to do with your mentality. It's time for your mind to be renewed.

Your trauma, abuse, and offense have taught you to self-sabotage. But the word of God will teach you how to possess the promise.

Your mentality matters. The word brain isn't in the Bible. It's all about the mind. The closest thing we get to the mind is a picture of a brain, but there is no picture of a mind because a mind has to do with your personality and soul. There's no picture of your soul. The closest you get is a picture of a brain, but the brain is not mentioned in the Bible. It's all about the mind. All of our brains look similar, but if there was a picture of our mind it would be very different. Every mind is as unique as your thumbprint. As a man thinks in his heart, so is he.

Psychology affects cardiology. How I think affects my heart. What you endure mentally affects the body physically, even your eating habits. Some people have suffered from so much emotional neglect that they have developed a food addiction. Emotional neglect causes the body to start yearning for emotion. When it yearns for emotion, you interpret it as hunger. You start overeating and becoming obese not because you love food, but because you need love and support. It is clinically proven that the mind affects the body. The enemy uses our trauma to hinder us from becoming what God wants us to be. Trauma can stunt your growth.

How you respond mentally to a situation at 8 years old is not the same way you should react to different situations at 20 or 60 years old. It isn't until you allow God to heal the trauma that you can have a proper mindset and outlook on life and people. The mind is so important. The children of Israel were in the battle for their lives, and their greatest battle was their minds. They were slaves, but in a single day, they came out of Egypt by their armies. They went from bakers to generals in a day. Now, that's a mental shift. Imagine someone asking them, "What's your military background?" An Israelite responds, "I bake cakes." They had zero military experience, yet God called them an army. The mental shift they had to make in a day went from bakers and slaves to free generals and soldiers. That is a drastic mental shift. It is similar to what happens after you come to God. You have been abused and told that you were nothing your whole life. But a Christian tells you, "Hey, you're a child of God; the Father loves you."

That's a shift that you got to make because, for 19 years, your daddy said he didn't love you. Now, you are walking this journey, trying to decipher how to live out the treasure God has entrusted you. As a PhD student, my professors warned me about the imposter syndrome. No matter how smart you are, you feel like an imposter. You feel that you do not belong. It's the same thing that happens whenever you come to God. God gives you a calling and a purpose, but you feel you don't belong. It is a mental shift.

One of the first things to overcome when God gives a promise is the feeling of inadequacy. If you cave into that feeling of inadequacy, you will sabotage what God is trying to bring you into. God tells them, "Go. Possess the land." They saw ourselves as grasshoppers. They were fully equipped and had a promise from God. The mind would not let them take hold of what was already given. God has given you a promise, but your mind keeps on pulling you back to what you were before. Every time God calls you to a new level, you must fight that feeling of being defined by yesterday.

In the wilderness, God supplied the children of Israel bread from heaven for 40 years. God gave them a miracle of preservation. The people were commanded to go out and gather at a specific rate daily. It was a miracle of survival. They could not survive the wilderness without this manna. God came into the middle of their wilderness and their trouble. Through his supernatural power, he gave them the ability to survive what most would not be able to survive. It was a miracle of survival. Has God ever supernaturally kept you from destruction and inevitable defeat? The trauma was supposed to kill you, but the Bread of Life preserved you. The abuse could have killed you, but God stepped in and preserved you. Thank God for manna. He provided you with just enough to keep going. The enemy tried to destroy you in your wilderness, but God nourished you and maintained you. You could have quit. You could have given up a long time ago. But something came down from heaven to preserve you. Manna was bread from heaven. That was the miracle of manna. God gave them just enough to keep on going. God gave them just what they needed. He gave them just enough to get through the next day. It's the miracle of survival. You were not supposed to become who you are today because of everything that happened in your family, but God sent a miracle to preserve you. You should be in an asylum with all that occurred in your church, but God is keeping your mind. That cult almost destroyed you, but God wouldn't let it happen. It is the miracle of manna. Manna was a supernatural provision for 40 years. The only thing about manna is that the children of Israel could not grab more than what was needed. They had a certain rate. There was a limit. It was just for survival, not for abundance. If you tried to get more, it was disobedience. If you tried to grab more than necessary, you would reap back worms and bacteria. The manna was there to just keep you. It was just to keep you until you got to the promise. But as soon as they tasted the corn of the promised land, the manna ceased. As soon as they tasted the future, the manna ceased. As soon as they got a taste of the future, the miracle of preservation ended.

Manna does not exist in the promised land. There is only an abundance of corn. In the Promised Land, you are not surviving off of "just enough" anymore. In the promise you can grab as much as you like. There is abundance all around you. How much do you want? You don't have to settle for a certain rate anymore. You can pray as long as you like. You get to worship as long as you like. You can have remaining joy. You don't have to worry about it being taken from you. The manna has ceased. The promise requires a new way of thinking. The manna way doesn't work in the promised land. That song used to always bring you to tears, but it puts you to sleep now. You have moved from manna territory into corn territory. The survival tactics do not work anymore because you have tasted the promise. You have tasted the future. You can't survive on just enough anymore. In the wilderness, God did everything for the children of Israel. They were not responsible for producing manna. That was God's responsibility. In the promised land, you are responsible for sowing and reaping corn. Now, it is you and God working together. God and therapy. God and accountability. God and resources. God and books. It's not survival anymore. There is an abundance of resources all around you. You can come out of that survival mindset and step into the opportunities laid before you. Their minds were so ingrained for 40 years on the manna of survival that when the manna ceased, they had to get their mind over the "just enough mentality." Just enough money to make it another week. Just enough friends. Just enough success to pay the bills. They had to get their mind over manna to go to the next level. Mind over the survival mindset. They had to get out of the survival mentality and step into possessing the land. They survived off of section 8 but were now moving into entrepreneurship. They had to get delivered from the mindset of manna. Because what was illegal during manna time is legal during corn time. What would get you chastised during manna season is encouraged in corn season. If they tried to go for more during manna, they got chastised for it. What are you doing? We're in the wilderness. We all get the same. That's enough. Everyone gets their certain rate. You can't get more. You were chastised. If you tried to get more of what God gave you, you would only get back worms and bacteria. If you are surrounded by people who constantly hold you back and show you all the dangers in the world, then that is your manna crowd. Manna crowds don't do well around corn. They love talking about the past, hurt, and pain but don't have a language for the future. When it is a nonstop blessing, they start feeling irrelevant in your life. They have to create problems in your life to be the solutions. They don't know how to rejoice and be joyful. They are stuck in the manna mentality. For some of y'all, it is tough for you to let go of what happened during manna season.

But if you cleave to the past, it can persecute the present. You say, "Oh, if I can just get my life back. If I can just get my stuff back." With this mentality your measurement is always behind you. Your mind is always on what is behind you. It's time to get your mind over manna. God is trying to give you a mentality of abundance. He did not come to just provide you with life. I am thankful that you survived and that you are still alive. But he wants to give you abundant life. What is before you is going to be a thousand times greater than what is behind you. Don't let the past persecute the future. Don't idolize the past so much that you miss the miracle of the present.

You got to get your mind over manna. Stop trying to live this life barely surviving. God is bringing you out of survival mode. It is time to possess the promise. You survived because you have a future. It is time to get our minds over manna and get our minds on a miracle.

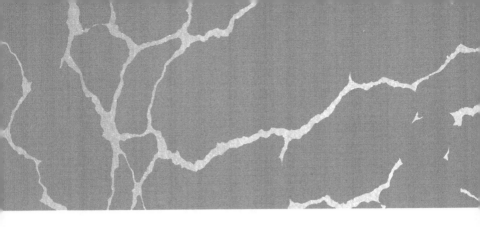

Power does not corrupt people; power reveals people. Little character flaws are unnoticeable in the shadows, but they become magnified when in a position of power. Your rough edges are a lot more dangerous as you climb higher. Allow God to take care of the little things in your life right now so that you can last.

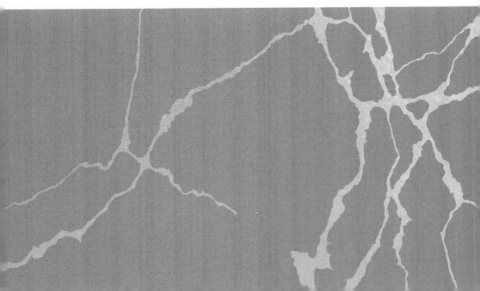

5

WASTED WOUNDS?

The woman conceived and bore a son, and when she saw that he was a fine child, she hid him three months. When she could hide him no longer, she took for him a basket made of bulrushes and daubed it with bitumen and pitch. She put the child in it and placed it among the reeds by the river bank.

EXODUS 2:2-3 ESV

was abused and beaten by my stepfather for the first 11 years of my life. I remember being kicked in my ribs and moving in constant pain and fear. I was desperately trying to appease someone who I thought was my biological father. I always wondered what I did to deserve it. Most survivors process trauma this way. Why would this happen to me? What was so wrong with me? Because abuse was regular to me, I became a glutton for punishment throughout my life. I did not run from pain. Instead, I ran to it because I believed that I deserved it. I was not disappointed when people rejected me or caused pain to me. My abuse had trained me to see myself in a negative light, but I can see the positive in everyone else. It took me years to understand that I was not the problem. For the first five years of my life, I could not speak English intelligibly. The trauma was so bad that it affected my speech. I babbled as a baby at 5 years old. My older sister had to interpret for me. Moses had his brother Aaron to interpret, and I had my sister. I stuttered, and I babbled in kindergarten.

My mom had to send me to a speech therapist for a year to teach me how to speak. A speech therapist at Highland Elementary in Eunice, LA, taught me for a year. Every week, she put a love in me for words and pronunciation. My speech therapist trained me to pronounce each word in great detail. One day, language finally clicked for me. I grew up speaking very proper English. I came out of my pain speaking correctly. I went out of my pain, speaking clearly. God did not create my abuse or my trauma, but he was able to use my story so that he could get glory. The change was so dramatic. Growing up in Louisiana, everyone wondered where I was from because I did not have a Louisiana accent.

God didn't create my pain, but He used my pain to prepare me to preach in the future. Pain prepared me to write in the future. From being in speech therapy, I developed a fascination with words. I got into poetry and writing. My love for Greek and Hebrew came out of my passion for words. My Masters in Biblical Exposition was achieved because of my love for words and, more importantly, God's words. The book you are reading presently was birthed out of this love for God, people, and words. Nothing that I went through has been wasted. Nothing that you have been through has been wasted. My infatuation with words allowed me to communicate in English, which became the foundation for me to learn other languages, such as Spanish. God used what the devil meant for evil for my good and the world's good. God was able to strategically use my suffering to bring him glory. He did not author my pain but pulled something beautiful out of it.

God is sovereign. Before he formed you in the womb, he knew you. No one can stop what God has for you. He will recycle everything he can to bring use and meaning out of the trauma. God can redeem anything. He can redeem the time you lost. Many people waste food every year because of the food's appearance. Consumers throw many fruits and vegetables away because they are not appealing to the eyes. Almost 12 billion pounds of food are thrown away every year in the

United States. We've become accustomed to having our produce be perfectly shaped; we like our fruit and vegetables to be symmetrical, color-corrected, and unblemished. Uglies Kettle Chips has made a profitable business by making kettle chips from discarded potatoes. They are helping farmers and donating some of the profits to fight global hunger. Uglies Kettle Chips has used over 25 million pounds of discarded "ugly" potatoes to use them for something more profitable. What others saw as waste, they recycled and repurposed to develop something powerful and even profitable. Don't waste your wound.

God wants to repurpose and recycle it to make your story even more remarkable, but this takes a shift in perspective. There is value in your story. You are still alive after the abuse, trauma, and offense. Don't sit in the pain; allow God to use the pain to rewrite your story. Rewrite the narrative. You are more than a conqueror. I am still drawing from my wound to produce writings and sermons ministering to millions of people yearly. There is something authentic about you using your pain to cultivate purpose within you and others. No one else has your story, but everyone can relate to your story. Your wound will not be wasted.

Moses' mother had to make a shift in her mindset. Instead of holding on to Moses to protect him, she realized that his only chance of survival was to let him go. Moses had a greater chance of survival being placed in a small ark among the reeds than in his mother's arms. Pharoah and his army were destroying every male child that was born. It was painful, but she had to release him. Moses' mother did not place him in the river. Many people like to think that Moses' mom put him in an ark and put him in the river. That's not what the Bible says. She actually placed Moses among the reeds.

This was not coincidental. God's hand was guiding her even during a traumatic experience. She had to let her child go for him to survive. There was something powerful about her placing him in the reeds. Whenever you study the life of Moses in-depth, you understand that his entire life would be spent dealing with these particular reeds alongside the Nile River. Throughout history they would break open these reeds. They would take out the inner bark from the reed. Then lay it down flat and spread it out. Finally, they would start writing on these reeds. They called those reeds "papyrus." That is where we get the word "paper." Every civilization worldwide came to Egypt to gather these reeds from the Nile River. The Nile River was the most prominent place in the world to get paper.

The Greek philosophers had to go to the Nile River and break off some reeds to make papyrus. The Greek philosophers used papyrus to create the ideal of philosophy. The Romans had to go to the Nile River to get papyrus to create their common law. Two Greek words were used for these reeds: papyrus and biblos. Biblos is where you get the word: Bible. The word Bible just means "the books." The books were made of papyrus. Much later, they would use leather, but that was a costly option to which the wealthy had access. They used "papyrus" from the Nile for mass writing because it was the most inexpensive commodity upon which to write. This is profound because the earliest writings came from those reeds that Moses was laid down in. Moses was inspired by the Holy Spirit to write the first five book of the Bible. The Pentateuch. The Torah. Genesis, Exodus, Leviticus, Numbers, and Deuteronomy. All these books were made from the reeds along the Nile River.

To continue writing God's words, Moses had to send people back to his experience. That had to go back to the Nile River to get another writing. He had to send them back to his moment of abandonment to produce another writing. He had to send people back to his first traumatic moment in childhood, to receive another writing. He had to continue sending people to his most traumatic moment to produce hope for the future. Moses spent his entire life writing about these same reeds that he had been laid down in as an infant. He received power and revelation out of some of his most vulnerable moments. Moses revisited his experience of pain but with a new mindset and perspective. He found a well of wisdom flowing out of his wound. He sent them back to his wound to receive a writing. Out of every wound comes a writing. Out of the gory comes a story. Out of the pain comes a plot. Out of the fire comes a foundation. He revisited the place of his wound to get fresh inspiration for writing. God gave him the words, but the reeds were the place of the wound.

Writings came out of the wound. Something powerful came out of the pain. Nothing that Moses went through, even down to the reeds, was wasted. He did not deny his experience; he integrated it into his story of overcoming. He repurposed his pain. Moses spoke of his pain with words filled with purpose, not bitterness. Nothing that you have been through has been wasted. Anything that you have gone through has not been wasted. There's a writing coming out of it. There's a new chapter coming out of it. There's fresh inspiration coming out of it. Moses was laid strategically in those reeds. He would spend his whole life writing on those reeds. The reeds that he babbled by he would later speak prophetically on.

The sovereignty of God is beautiful. The place that he felt abandoned as a child. The place where he felt rejected as a child. The place where he felt most fearful. God still used to produce another writing. There is writing coming out of your wound. No matter how bad or unfortunate your life has been. Somehow, God's going to get the glory out of this. You may not understand it now, but you will realize it later. It doesn't make sense now, but God is writing a masterpiece with your life. Your life is going to become someone else's reason to continue living. There is a writing coming out of this.

There's a new chapter coming out of this. Moses had to send them back where he felt abandoned, rejected, and alone. Moses spent his entire life working with these reeds from the Nile River. Think about the irony of Moses' life. Before Moses was born Israel cried out for a deliverer. The daughter of Pharaoh comes and gets him from these reeds. He wasn't even named by his mother. He was named by Pharoah's daughter. But even those moments, God used. She named him Moses because he was drawn out of the water.

Interestingly, Moses would later draw an entire nation out of the water (the Red Sea). Pharoah's daughter raised Moses in Pharoah's house. The children of Israel were searching for deliverance and God answered their prayers by raising their deliverer in the enemy's house. God used the enemy to teach Moses how to conquer nations. Nothing you have been through shall be wasted. God is sovereign. Thank you, Pharoah. Thank you for teaching Moses how to lead a nation. Pharoah taught him how to develop an army. Pharoah taught Moses how to conquer land. The enemy was preparing Moses to possess the promise land. God allowed the enemy to teach him warfare and strategy. It was under the tutelage of Pharoah that Moses learned how to write. He received the best education in Egypt. Those instructors taught him military strategy. God used the enemy to teach Moses how to possess kingdoms and conquer nations. Moses thought he had wasted 40 years of his life in Pharoah's house, but God was using the adverse circumstances to develop his prophet for his own purposes.

God answered their prayer by raising a baby in the enemy's house. God used adversity to teach him how to conquer. This is what God does. God can use your enemy. He can use your difficult upbringing to produce amazing things. He may not have created your pain, but he has the power to repurpose it. God uses your circumstances to bring out the best in you. He uses life's difficulties to bring out who you're called to be.

God did it with David. God told Samuel to go to Jesse's house because God said, "I found a man after my own heart." Samuel goes to Jesse's house, and he doesn't find a man. He finds a boy, but there was a man in the boy, but God had to raise up a giant to get the man out of the boy. Your giant is working for you because it's bringing something out of you that you didn't even know was there. David thought he would be a shepherd, but his giant showed him that there was a king in there somewhere. He thought he was a shepherd, but his adversity taught him that there was royalty in him. David thought he was nothing, but his giant showed him he was something. His father and brothers trained him to watch sheep, but his giant trained him to watch over a nation. Thank you, giant. You didn't know that you had that in there. But with the hell that he put you through, you discovered that there was greatness within you. Before he met Goliath, he was equipped with a sling. After he meets Goliath, he is equipped with a giant sword. God can use adversity to develop your muscles. The pain brought the man out of the boy. Before the pain, he could only carry a sling; after the pain, he was man enough to carry a giant sword.

The difficulty brought the best out of him and equipped him to do more extraordinary things. After he kills the giant, they sing, "Saul has slain his thousands and David has slain ten thousand." David only killed one person, Goliath, but they are beginning to sing that he conquered 10,000 people. If you only knew how many victories that your giant was connected to. He killed one giant and he immediately received thousands of victories. Once you defeat this giant of depression. This giant of doubt. This giant of fear. This giant of trauma. This giant of offense. This giant of abuse. You are going to reap thousands of victories.

In the Ancient Near Eastern custom, if you did not want a bloody war. You brought out the best man from both camps. Whoever won this one-on-one battle received victory over the opponent's thousands of soldiers. One representative on each side of the camp would represent the whole nation, and when they fought, whoever won defeated the entire nation. That's why they sang, "David has slain tens of thousands." With one victory, he defeated the entire host.

You're up against something, and you feel the resistance to be so heavy. You are going to defeat this giant by the grace of God. Your family will receive the fruit of this victory for generations to come. They will not have to deal with the abuse like you did because you defeated it. You brought forth a writing out of the wound. You produced resources out of your rejection. You are producing books and businesses out of your bruises. Out of your mess, God has made you into a mentor. Don't look at your adversity as if you have been targeted. Look at your adversity as a teacher. This is the change of mindset needed. Nothing in your life will be wasted. The wound was not a waste. Writing and worship were the twins that were birthed out of your wound.

Pharoah was killing all of the male children and throwing them into the Nile River.

But Pharaoh couldn't kill Moses. Pharaoh had to watch the deliverer of Israel being raised right under his nose. Pharoah was carrying the deliverance of Israel to his crib. No matter how many babies Pharaoh killed, he couldn't kill this baby. Moses was placed in these reeds at the beginning of his life. Later, he delivered over three million people across the Red Sea. They walked through the Red Sea on dry ground. The English word "Red Sea" in Hebrew is actually "The Sea of Reeds." In Hebrew it is The Sea of Reeds. It all makes sense now, doesn't it? Moses had to go through his own reed experience so he could identify with others in their reed experience. He has to endure his personal reed moment because he would walk millions of people through their own reed moment. Moses did not endure his pain in vain. He went through it so that he could help someone else. You didn't go through it just for you. You didn't cry just for you. You didn't weep just for you. You didn't battle just for you. This is bigger than you think. You are currently battling so that your kids never have to fight that battle. You are battling so that your family never has to fight that battle. You're battling so that your church, community, and company never have to fight that battle.

You are getting a victory in your own personal reed experience to help others in their reed experience. Moses related to them because he felt alone before. Moses related to them because at three months old, he didn't know what he was going to do. He went through his reed experience to help three million people through their reed experience. God is sovereign. God uses what looks like a coincidence to put a beautiful story together. There is a writing coming out of this. You are getting delivered because God will use you to deliver others.

Because of the abuse that I suffered as a child and throughout my life, I can preach and write deliverance to the hurting. Any person who's been abused, traumatized, or hurt. I pray that I can be a visual example to you that there is hope. There is abundant life, even after abuse. If God can mend me then God can heal you. If He can mend a babbling five-year-old like me, I'm here to show you that He can mend your broken pieces together. But I personally believe that God will do greater with you. That is my prayer for your life.

If God can help me to overcome the Complex PTSD and PTSD then he will help you. If God can help me overcome a chipped tooth and being punched in the face several times. If God can help me heal from being locked outside the house multiple times for 12-14 hours without food or water. If God can help me overcome this psychological trauma, he can do the same with you. I went through a reed experience, and I didn't go through it for myself. I went through it to help millions of people survive and overcome to come out of their own reed experience. Moses' exodus from the water led to Israel's exodus from Egypt. You know what it feels like to be weary. You know what it feels like to cry and feel insignificant. You know what it feels like to battle suicidal thoughts, but you survived your reed experience to help a world that's going through its own reed experience. It's not just for you, it's for the world.

I know that your greatest fear is wasted years. You feel that you wasted time in workplaces and churches and so much time.

God's writing something in you. You may want to summarize your life and write loss, but God writes loved. God said in his word, "I will send my spirit to write my law upon your hearts." Look at everything written in your heart from your childhood. Look at all that's been written on your heart and your life. God says, "When I pour out my spirit upon your life, I am washing that heart and I am putting my law on that heart. Wherever you tried to write 'problem,' I replaced it with 'promise.' You are my epistle."

Isn't it amazing that it says we overcome the enemy by the blood of the lamb and by the word of our testimony? That's incredible because the blood is enough. By the blood, we win. By the blood, we win, but he says, "You overcome by the blood of the lamb and by the word of your testimony." In other words, I don't want you to just win. I want you to talk and tell the devil he wasn't close. God wants you to talk trash to the devil! I know you talk trash against your most hated sports team. It's time to talk trash to the one person that we are allowed to hate: the devil. This is what it means when he says through him that we are more than conquerors.

Stop questioning God this way: "God, why, why, why?" Instead, ask, "How will you get glory out of this?" When you feel discouraged, I'm telling you, you went through it to help others. Jesus couldn't change the world. You got to hear this, guys. He could not change the world from heaven.

Before the children of Egypt went through the Sea of Reeds, they spoiled the Egyptians. They took utensils, money, and many things out of Egypt. They used the spoils of Egypt for the service of the tabernacle. Spoils are coming out of this reed experience, and it will be used for the purpose of God. Those utensils in Egypt became the utensils that were used in the tabernacle. Those things from Egypt became consecrated and dedicated to the service of God. They didn't spend all their lives questioning, "Why were we in Egypt for 430 years?" You know what they just did? They used what they got from Egypt for the service of the Lord. God can use it. God didn't create your pain. God didn't put you through that. The enemy did. Life did, but God is willing to use it for His glory.

You need to stop trying to end your story and put the pen back into the hand of God because He's not done writing. You tried to hide the pen and put it in your pocket to end your story. Don't try to end your story like Tamar did. Tamar tried to end her story because of what she went through.

Tamar was the king's daughter, and a tragedy happened to her. She was raped by someone she trusted. She was taken advantage of by her relative. I am surprised that not many speak of Tamar's story. Not many discuss the pain of sexual abuse and rape. Tamar had a coat of many colors, but no one speaks of her coat of many colors. After she went through that traumatic moment the Bible states,

> *"Then he called his servant that ministered unto him, and said, Put now this woman out from me, and bolt the door after her. And she had a garment of divers colours upon her: for with such robes were the king's daughters that were virgins apparelled. Then his servant brought her out, and bolted the door after her. And Tamar put ashes on her head, and rent her garment of divers colours that was on her, and laid her hand on her head, and went on crying. And Absalom her brother said unto her, Hath Amnon thy brother been with thee? but hold now thy peace, my sister: he is thy brother; regard not this thing. So Tamar remained desolate in her brother Absalom's house"* (2 Samuel 13:17-20 KJV).

Tamar remained desolate in her brother Absalom's house. Tamar had a coat of many colors that the king placed upon her as a form of distinction. This coat was a sign that she was a king's daughter. Tamar did not feel like a king's daughter whenever the tragedy happened. She felt naked and dirty. She felt ashamed and sick inside. She replayed the event over and over in her head. She thought to herself, "Maybe I was too trusting. I shouldn't have served him. I shouldn't have been so naïve." It wasn't her fault. She got abused while serving King David. Imagine being abused after just trying to obey the King of Kings. King David sent her to serve her brother, but the brother took advantage of her innocence. She never looked at the kingdom the same again. Tamar wondered how the king could have allowed something like this to happen to her. She did not feel like a king's daughter. She did not feel chosen. She felt broken and damaged. She felt like damaged goods. To understand how she felt we must understand how God views rape.

> *"But if a man find a betrothed damsel in the field, and the man force her, and lie with her: then the man only that lay with her shall die. But unto the damsel thou shalt do nothing; there is in the damsel no sin worthy of death: for as when a man riseth against his neighbour, and slayeth him, even so is this matter: For he found her in the field, and the betrothed damsel cried, and there was none to save her* (Deuteronomy 22:25-27 KJV).

I want this to sink in; God compares rape to murder. When someone is raped, God sees it as a murder being committed. That is not something to take lightly. This is not something to push under the rug. This is serious. It is the same thing in God's eyes. It is as if a murder was committed because something dies in the life of that victim that cannot be revived by human efforts. Only God can heal that person and restore them. Imagine something dying within you, but you are still alive. It makes you want to die. You feel like dying because no one understands. They want you to get over it quickly. But it feels like you are carrying death. Only God can reach into your soul and breathe life into you. I am thankful for professional help and a helpful community, but do not underestimate the God factor. Imagine your offender getting away with murder. It doesn't feel good. Imagine having to see your abuser every workday or every Sunday. It is difficult to move on from something like that. It is easy for bitterness and resentment to creep in. Tamar's life was turned upside down, and Absalom told her not to worry. He told her to be silent. After you have been abused, everyone tells you to hold your peace. They want you to hold your peace to keep the peace. The problem is that everyone goes on with their lives while you are the one who continues to suffer. Don't hold your peace. Come out of the prison of fear. You have a testimony that needs to be shared. Make them uncomfortable. If they felt comfortable taking advantage of you, you should feel comfortable proclaiming what they did. No one heard you cry out at that moment, but they will hear you now. Not out of revenge but out of testimony. If your testimony makes them uncomfortable, oh well. However, the unfortunate thing in Tamar's story is that she internalizes her pain. She allowed the shame to eat away at her.

Something died in her that day. She had a coat of many colors, but she did the unthinkable. She rent her coat. She tore her garment. That garment was her identity. She was a king's daughter. She didn't feel like a daughter anymore. She rent her coat. She felt that God was done with her. She thought that the king didn't care about her. Tamar did not believe that she could serve the king anymore. She tore her coat and remained desolate in her brother's house. She never left his home. She cut herself off from the king and everyone else. She tore her identity. She rent her coat and hid away from the world. This is why no one speaks of Tamar; she ended her own story. She had a coat of many colors, just like Joseph had, but we speak of Joseph's coat of many colors, not hers. Do you know why we never speak of her coat? It's because she destroyed her own coat. She ended her own story. She did not allow God the opportunity to turn it around. She did not give God time to bring a testimony out of the pain. She didn't allow God to take the pen out of her hand. God would have written a beautiful redemption story. Tamar could have been another hero mentioned in the pages of Scripture that overcame insurmountable odds. But she prematurely ended her story. We don't know how long she lived afterward. But I would never want it said over my life that I died at 11 years old and was buried at 95 years old. I don't want to end my own story early. Your trauma does not have the authority to end your story. Only you can end your story. We understand her pain and her suffering, but as long as she was alive, she had a purpose.

This is why we never speak of her. She destroyed her own coat. The reason we speak of Joseph is because he never rent his own coat. He never destroyed his own identity. Because he never rent his own coat, it allowed God to get glory out of what happened to him. He never destroyed his own identity. The enemy rent his coat; he didn't destroy his own coat. There is a difference between you rending your coat and the enemy rending your coat. If you tear your coat, you end your story. But if the enemy tears your coat, your story is just getting started. Whenever the enemy rends your coat, it means that you have outgrown it. When the enemy rends your coat from you, you have outgrown it, and God is now measuring you for a new coat. If the enemy tries to destroy your coat, God will immediately start measuring you for a new coat. They rent his first coat, which was the coat of promise. They tore it from him and got him measured for a new coat when they rent it from him. The second coat was the coat of process he got in Potiphar's house. In Potiphar's house, Potiphar's wife rent that coat from him. She rent the coat of process, but God began to measure Joseph for a new coat. The last coat was the coat of the palace which his enemy would give him. That was the coat of fulfillment; no devil in hell can take away the coat of fulfillment from your life.

God starts getting you measured for a new coat when the enemy rends your coat. Jesus Christ was God in the flesh. He left the splendors of heaven. He left the walls of Jasper and the pearly gates. He left the streets of gold and the worship of angels. Jesus Christ robed Himself in flesh. Jesus came in a coat of flesh. He walked around for 33 years in a coat of flesh. Fully God and fully man. While he was in that coat of flesh, he was crucified. On the cross, they began to rend his coat. They picked up a spear and rent his coat. But when they tore his coat, it got him measured for a resurrection coat. The devil still wishes that he never tore Jesus Christ coat. The enemy is going to wish that he never tore your coat. 3 days later, the devil discovered the story was not over. It was just the beginning. The past was buried, and the future began to arise. The enemy is going to wish he never touched you and your family. Jesus Christ had his coat torn but got measured for a resurrection coat.

They measure me for a new coat whenever I go to the suit store. Whenever they start measuring me for a new suit, they first tell me, "Victor, stretch your arms out." They say, "Victor, I want you to put your feet together." They say, "Victor, let me put the pins in you. I am measuring you for a new coat." Well, they stretched Jesus's arms out. Then they put His feet together. Then they put the pins in Him, which got Him measured for a new coat. It's time to take off the spirit of heaviness and put on the garment of praise. It's time to put on the coat of praise. Shake off the heaviness; your story is not over. The devil thought your destiny was being murdered, but with God, you were just being measured. If your enemy only knew that a new coat was waiting on you, he would not have torn your old one. If the enemy only knew that you would become better after the depression. After the trauma. After the abuse. After the struggle. After the offense. You are not tearing your coat. God is not done with you. God is not done writing your story. A new coat is coming upon you while you are reading this book.

God is still writing your story. There is writing coming out of your wound. Take the pen out of your hand. You have tried to write "The End." But God is writing, "The Den." He just rearranged the order of the words. He repurposes the letters. It is not the e-n-d. It is just the d-e-n. What you thought was the end of your story was just the end of a chapter called "The Den." Allow God to rearrange the letters. It wasn't the end; it was just the den. You were in a den full of lions, but you know how the story ended for Daniel. I am so thankful Daniel didn't end his story in that den of lions. At that moment, he looked forsaken by God. But thank God that he did not end his story. God delivered him and gave him influence. God used him mightily after everyone thought it was the end. It was just a den. Give God what you believe in the end. God will turn your end into a den. Put the pen back in God's hands. This is just a cliffhanger when you think the hero is about to die. Give God the pen back. He is the author. He is the original creative. He is the producer. You are coming out of that den with a new coat. Give God the pen. We lift our hands in worship because we're giving the pen back to God. You are surrendering the pen. You are giving him complete control to write what he wants to write. There's a story coming out of this. The greatest masterpieces have a trial and tragedy in them. A story without trial and tragedy is meaningless. There has to be a moment of conflict and pain. Why? No story is complete without an antagonist. No story is complete without an enemy. No story is complete without opposition. No story is complete without it. It's a masterpiece. There's a masterpiece coming out of this mess. You are going to get fresh inspiration out of this. I can feel your mindset beginning to change. You might as well get a book out of what you have been through. This is the stuff they make books out of. This is the stuff that they make entertainment and movies out of. You even told friends, "Man, my life is like a movie." There is a writing coming out of this.

God saw a little boy crying in the closet and said, "Victor, there's a writing coming out of this." I am not the only one who has suffered abuse. This book will help other kids who were victims of traumatic moments. There is a writing coming out of this. People are walking through the Sea of Reeds, and you need your reed experience to get them through.

I am writing to you with my new coat on. I can testify that it's not over. I wanted to end my life in that closet. I am so glad that I didn't. This coat is comfy. I wanted to disappear and hide for the rest of my life like Tamar. I am so happy that I didn't. God is not done. God has a plan for you. Don't close the book. He's still writing, and a masterpiece will come out of it. It's not over. There's a writing coming out of it. It's going to bless the world. It's not just for you; it's for them. It's time to understand the potential within you, in every scar that is a story. It is time to share it. It's not over for you. Let's move forward in our healing journey. Not only will God give you new writing, but he will also bless you with a new language.

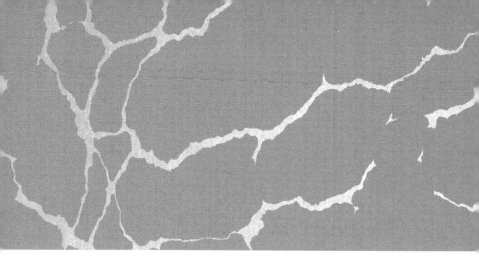

It is difficult to find the right words when processing pain. If you cannot find the right words, invent them. Allow your pain to push you into innovation and creativity. Allow your suffering to create a new language.

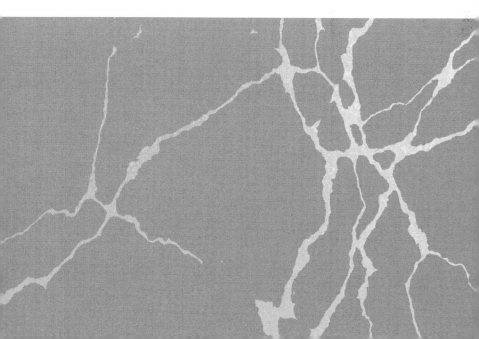

6

THE LANGUAGE OF SCARS

"But Thomas, one of the twelve, called Didymus, was not with them when Jesus came. The other disciples therefore said unto him, We have seen the Lord. But he said unto them, Except I shall see in his hands the print of the nails, and put my finger into the print of the nails, and thrust my hand into his side, I will not believe.

JOHN 20:24-25 KJV

There is something about pain that doesn't need words of expression. You can look into somebody's eyes and notice if they are in pain, or you can look at how someone walks and notice if they are in pain. There's something about pain that has its own unique language. Most researchers say that 70% of our communication is nonverbal. There's something about experiencing physical, emotional, and spiritual pain that communicates with every human heart.

God has put a language into man's heart that no other animal or creature can understand. Scientists argue that humans are the only mammals that cry tears out of emotion. Other animals may have tears, but human tears have meaning. There is a language of pain that doesn't need to be communicated verbally.

There's something about pain that is communicated subtly. In the Old Testament there was an important woman named Hagar. Hagar was pregnant with Ishmael and because she was pregnant with Ishmael, there was contention between her and Sarah. Sarah is in a position of authority, so she makes Hagar's life miserable. Hagar ran away after being treated horribly by Sarah. She did not sign up for this life of heartache. She was brought into the middle of Abraham and

Sarah's feud. She ran away. On her journey, she got lost in the wilderness. She had nothing to drink. She was pregnant and alone. She was about to die. Without uttering a word, an angel showed up by her side. The angel said, "You are going to name this child Ishmael, for the Lord has heard your affliction." She never uttered a word. She did not pray to God. Yet the angel declared that the Lord had heard her affliction. The Lord heard her pain.

Pain has a voice. Pain has its own language. "The Lord has heard your affliction." Hagar never prayed to God, but her pain spoke on her behalf. She didn't even have a relationship with the Lord; she was an Egyptian. She never talked to God, but her scar spoke up for her. She was by herself and about to die from dehydration, but the angel said, "The Lord has heard your affliction." When you do not know what to say to God, your pain speaks on your behalf. God doesn't wait for you to form the words with your mouth. No. He comes and visits where you are, and he delivers to you. He doesn't wait for you to get it all together. He comes where you are.

He doesn't wait for you to get the prayer language just right. He doesn't wait for you to get the KJV language just right. He doesn't wait until you read a whole chapter in the Bible or a whole book in the Bible. No. When he sees his daughter in trouble. When he sees his son going through a situation. He does not just wait for you to say something before he starts moving because your scar is already saying something. God says, "I know they haven't prayed to me yet, but I see them suffering right now and I'm going to heal and help them come out of this better. Their relationship with me may not be ideal right now, but I won't allow the enemy to destroy them. I will do whatever it takes to deliver and bring them out better than they went in."

A scar has its own language. Pain has its own language. Hagar was an Egyptian. She was accustomed to worshiping false gods, but God could not ignore the sound of her pain. Even when you cannot form words, your tears talk.

Even when I can't form the words, God sees the pain you are going through and chooses to comfort you. Even when you don't feel like talking. Have you ever been through something where you don't even want to talk to anybody? You don't even want to laugh. You don't wish to pretend. You don't even want to fellowship. You just want to go home and go back under those covers and go to bed because you're still under the weight of depression. God doesn't pass you by and say, "Hey, whenever you're ready to pray, I'll help you." But my pain begins to come to his ears and he says, "I got a word for you." Pain has its own language.

God is a God of consolation. The Greek word for consolation is paraklesis which means "to comfort, encourage, and give a holy urging." God not only comforts you with his presence, but he also comes alongside you to encourage you when you are in pain. To comfort means the existence of pain. No pain or trouble? Then there is no need to comfort. Psychologists are studying a phenomenon that happens whenever someone goes through a traumatic experience. They call it, "The Third Man Syndrome." They have studied people stranded in the wilderness with broken legs for many days. They studied people who had been stranded in the ocean for months. People who have endured trauma while going on an adventure. People who experienced a traumatic moment where they felt that they were about to die. All of these people testified that when they thought they were about to die that an unseen presence came alongside them to encourage them and even direct them to safety. This unseen presence came alongside them and encouraged them not to give up. They had no one around them. They were abandoned. They had no support, but an unseen presence came alongside them to encourage them on their journey. A voice spoke to them and encouraged them to not give up. This presence encouraged them after a near-death experience. The presence directed them to safety and gave practical advice. The voice told them, "Don't give up now. You have to try." They call it, "The Third Man Syndrome." We call it, "The Fourth Man in the Fire." They call it an unseen presence. We call it Jesus Christ. Those who endured trauma and did not know what to say or what to pray. The comforter came alongside them to encourage them. Their pain reached heaven's ears and pulled God's presence down. When you go through your trauma, you are not alone. It is God that has kept you from giving up. When you wanted to commit suicide, there was a voice that came to you and told you that you were going to survive that situation. God gave you strength in a moment of weakness. He is the fourth man in the fire of those three Hebrew boys. He is with you in the fire.

> *"And the Lord said, I have surely seen the affliction of my people which are in Egypt, and have heard their cry by reason of their taskmasters; for I know their sorrows; And I am come down to deliver them out of the hand of the Egyptians, and to bring them up out of that land unto a good land and a large, unto a land flowing with milk and honey…"* (Exodus 3:7-8 KJV).

Israel did not just pray for a deliverer. Israel cried out for a deliverer. God told Moses that he heard the cry of his people. God responds to tears. Your tears have a language that God hears. Whenever your words fall short, your tears make up the difference. God cannot ignore the cry of his child. Your child does not have to understand English before you feed him/her. When they cry, you know what they need. Your 5-month-old child does not have the language of humanity perfected, but everyone understands a cry. You will feed them or put them to sleep so that they can rest. There is something about a cry that pulls comfort out of an individual. If a child is crying by themselves in the middle of the store, watch how fast adults gather around the child to comfort it. A cry softens the hardest of hearts.

Although God heard Hagar's affliction, he did not fully understand her affliction. He was in heaven. He could not resonate with that level of hurt. He is abstract. He's in the heavenly of heavenlies. God is being worshiped all day by angels. He is walking on streets of gold. He's surrounded by the walls of jasper. He's on the throne. He is being worshiped all day. He is being worshiped in all of eternity. Although he heard her pain, he could not fully understand or resonate with it. There's nothing that he could do to relate.

This was the challenge in the Old Testament. God was so great, but he was unrelatable. He was so powerful, but we had no access to him. He could not fully relate to my tears because God never cried in the Old Testament. He never wept. We don't know what God's tears were like in the Old Testament because he didn't shed any. He was just a God of covenant. A God of laws. A God of obedience. But he could not relate to pain. He could only hear it. He just couldn't understand it fully. In the Old Testament, God could not relate to us in that way because he didn't have a body. He's a spirit.

God is a spirit. Those who worship him must worship him in spirit and truth. He is a spirit. He did not understand the battle that these people were having while trying to obey him. He just gave the law, and he expected them to obey. He had to become flesh to relate to us. He had to feel. We needed a high priest who could be touched by the feelings of our infirmities. We needed him to feel our pain in order to truly understand our struggle.

He couldn't feel us; he could only hear us in the Old Testament. He heard what we said, but he didn't feel what we said. He had not been through anything like that. He didn't know what anxiety felt like. He didn't know what depression felt like. He didn't know what pain felt like. He didn't know what that felt like. He could hear us but could not really understand our daily battle until he robed himself in the flesh. The fullness of God came in the man Christ Jesus. Born of the Virgin Mary, fully God and fully man, the God-man, the theanthropos. We needed his humanity to access his divinity. We needed his humanity to access the miraculous. We needed his humanity to tap into the kingdom. It was only by him becoming flesh that you and I are able to be here today because his god-ness and his man-ness are what was needed to get us into the deliverance. The Bible says, "Without the shedding of blood, there can be no remission of sin." God purchased the church with his own blood.

I'm so thankful for the New Testament because I see God in constant fights, that his god-ness does not negate fights. That helps me because no matter how spiritual I am, that doesn't mean that I won't ever be in some type of battle, that the struggle is not a sign of my distance from God, that the battle is not a sign of my own depravity. After all, Jesus, being a perfect man, was in a constant battle.

It made me shed a tear when I saw him finally shed a tear when he wept over Lazarus. "Jesus wept" is the shortest scripture in the Bible, but I weep reading it. He finally understood what it meant to cry. I thank God for hearing my cry, but here he is, feeling my cry. Whenever I saw him being rejected by his family, I said, "Wow, I'm not alone. We're not alone." God is relatable in the New Testament. He could not relate to and understand their pain in the Old Testament. Everything that you have endured and felt in your life, Jesus felt in his 33-year earthly body. He overcame it. He endured and overcame everything you're dealing with. Because he overcame it, now I can put my trust in him so I can overcome it as well. That's why he went through it. He went through it for us.

Jesus showed himself to the disciples, but somehow Thomas showed up late to the prayer meeting. He said, "Except I see in his hands the print of the nails and put my finger into the print of the nails and thrust my hand into his side, I will not believe." Thomas said, "I will not believe in his resurrection until I see a scar somewhere." Thomas did not understand the resurrection language; he only understood scar language. He could only understand someone who had been through something. He wanted to see the scars.

Finally, after eight days, Jesus came, and he said, "Reach hither thy finger and behold my hands and reach hither thy hand and thrust it into my side and be not faithless, but believing." This text gives us a glimpse into God's heart, with all the power of God that Jesus had. Jesus healed thousands of people in his ministry. He healed lepers. These lepers had so many scars on them. They had deep wounds that he healed. God cleansed them and even made them whole. A leper came back and worshiped, and God made him whole. There was no remnant of scars upon that leper. He made it as if the pain never happened. God did such a work within the leper. He took care of the leper's scars. Yet, whenever Jesus resurrected with all power in his hands; he left the scars behind. He was in his resurrected body, but he did not want to rid himself of the scars on his hands and side. He had the power to take his own scars away, but he did not want to. He wants to keep the scars because the scars are his language of relatability. Jesus said, "Give me my life back, but don't take my scar away." He got the keys to death, hell, and the grave with scars.

Jesus did not have to have scars on his hands. He didn't have to have scars on his feet. He didn't have to have a scar on his side. He didn't have to have that. Why would you leave that? In his scars were the language of relatability. He was alive but scarred. The scars did not mean that he was weak. The scars meant that he survived insurmountable odds. In every scar, there is a story. The scar means that whatever came against you didn't kill you. The scar means you learned to heal no matter how deep the cut was. No matter how deep they pierced you. No matter how deep they hurt you. The scar means that you defeated whatever was trying to defeat you. The scar tells the story. The scar testifies that what you went through did not destroy you. You were able to heal from an impossible situation. He wanted to leave the scars behind. Jesus said, "Give me my life but leave the scars behind. Give me my body, but leave the scars behind. I'll resurrect out the tomb, but just don't take the scar away." He did not want to lose his relatability language. No matter how much power he had, the scars were the bridge.

I've got scars on my body from different surgeries that I've gone through. I've got an ugly scar on the side of my leg after tearing my lateral ligament while playing basketball. I have a scar on my right knee from tearing my lateral meniscus. I have a scar on my eye from a basketball injury. I still have the scars. Anybody in humanity would love to say, "God, take the scar away." After my surgeries, they gave me Bio Oil to try to eliminate the presence of scars. But God wanted to ensure he kept the print in his hands. He wanted to keep the scar on his side so you never forget what he did for you. He did not want you to forget how much he loves you.

Every scar reveals a place of vulnerability. The scars show that someone got through the barrier. The scars reveal that God is capable of feeling and that God is capable of being hurt. God was abused on that cross. They played games around his cross while he was dying. They mocked him and beat him. God endured abuse for you, and he left the scar behind to prove it. No one has ever been abused like that. They spat on him. None of us have ever endured this level of misuse. They put those three nails in his hand. But I am thankful for those three nails. With those three nails, he began to knit something beautiful for our lives. He made a tapestry of redemption and restoration with three nails. God began to knit a recovery in your life. God began to knit his love with those three nails. He used a scarlet thread and three nails to display his love for us. What a beautiful tapestry. Three nails from man and the blood of Jesus Christ. Can you hear the scars speaking of his love for you right now? If you cannot hear God's voice, look at his scars. If you can't hear his voice, just think of his scars. The scars will start talking back to you. After having nails in his hands for some time, he would lose blood, and the hands would start closing. It was a literal death grip. No one can pluck you from his hands. On that cross, he put a death grip on your life. With that death grip, the scars scream, "I love you! You are mine forever." What he accomplished on that cross was to make sure no enemy could ever pluck you out of his hands. No emotion, no sickness, no anxiety, no fear. What can separate us from the love of God? Nothing can separate us from his love. No abuse. No trauma. No offense. No toxic relationship. No dysfunctional upbringing. The scars are speaking. The scars tell me that there is hope for me.

Jesus performed many miracles before Thomas' eyes, but Thomas had a difficult time believing. There were times when Jesus said, "If you don't believe me, believe me for the work's sake." To Thomas, he says, "If you don't believe me, believe me for the scar's sake."

> *"Then saith he to Thomas, Reach hither thy finger, and behold my hands; and reach hither thy hand, and thrust it into my side: and be not faithless, but believing. And Thomas answered and said unto him, My Lord and my God. Jesus saith unto him, Thomas, because thou hast seen me, thou hast believed: blessed are they that have not seen, and yet have believed. And many other signs truly did Jesus in the presence of his disciples, which are not written in this book: But these are written, that ye might believe that Jesus is the Christ, the Son of God; and that believing ye might have life through his name"* (John 20:27-31 KJV).

The scar was a sign. The scars were a sign to provoke belief. When Thomas saw the scars, he said, "My Lord and my God!" He confessed that Jesus Christ was God after he saw the scars. The scars ignited belief. It was the language of relatability. Some people will not believe in God until they understand that God bled for them. People do not care what you know until they know how much you care. People do not care how much you know until they know how much you bled. Most people are thankful that God is the creator, but they want to know what pain he went through for them.

I've come to write on behalf of God's scars. The scars say that God is not done with you.

It was more than a historical moment. It was an eternal moment.

When we put Jesus there because of our sins, think about any sin you've ever committed in your life, every sin, he paid the price. He thought of each and every one of us on that cross.

The nailed, scarred hands didn't hurt you. The people who hurt you are not God. Tune your ears to his scars.

You were a victim. You didn't deserve what happened to you. I'm just asking you, on behalf of the scars, not to blame God. He is the one trying to heal you. The trauma you endured, you were a victim. That was not supposed to happen to you.

Can you hear the scars speaking? He loves you. No mistake you've made can stop him from loving you. Hear the scars talk, he understands you. Your scars have made you relatable to the world. Show them your scars. Do not be ashamed of your story. His scars have given you a testimony. Because of His scars, you have a future.

Some circumstances do not change; they remain the same. Your mind must be renewed by the Spirit in order to learn how to navigate the situation in a godly and successful manner. Whenever God does not change your circumstances, it means that he is changing you. What God is doing in you is much greater than anything that the enemy has done to you.

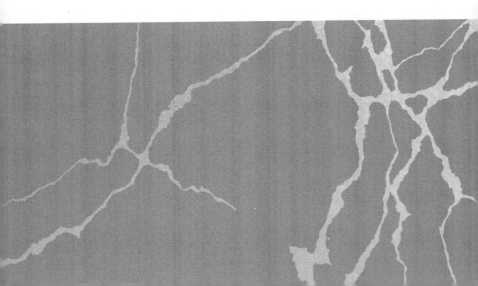

7

THE FORCE OF THE FUTURE

And Jacob was left alone; and there wrestled a man with him until the breaking of the day. And when he saw that he prevailed not against him, he touched the hollow of his thigh; and the hollow of Jacob's thigh was out of joint, as he wrestled with him. And he said, Let me go, for the day breaketh. And he said, I will not let thee go, except thou bless me. And he said unto him, What is thy name? And he said, Jacob. And he said, Thy name shall be called no more Jacob, but Israel: for as a prince hast thou power with God and with men, and hast prevailed.

GENESIS 34:24-28 KJV

Jacob was raised in a dysfunctional family. He was raised in a dysfunctional family because Rebecca loved Jacob, but Isaac loved Esau. Jacob and Esau were twins. They were brothers. But the mother loved Jacob, and the father loved Esau. That is the definition of a dysfunctional family. This dynamic gives birth to performance-driven relationships. Jacob was trying to get the approval of his father by his performance. Esau was trying to get his mother's approval through his performance. This dynamic birthed a competition between brothers. They were jealous of one another's connection with their parent. Children should not have to earn their parent's love. Suppose a child has to earn their parent's love. In that case, the child develops perfectionist tendencies, hindering their growth and development. Jacob's family was performance-based. It was highly traumatic for Jacob because no matter how hard he tried, his father would not show him attention. No matter how hard he worked, dad was not interested. Isaac loved Esau's deer meat that he took in from hunting, but Jacob dwelled in the house. Jacob tried his best to get his dad's approval but to no avail. He is trying to get that love, but it is not coming. It is traumatic to not receive love from a parent.

No matter how many times my stepdad said that he did not want me, I refused to believe him. I would work hard at trying to please him and perform. But the more I achieved, the worse the rejection was. His favorite soda was root beer. I went with my mom to the store and picked him up a case of root beer with my own money as a surprise. I was excited to hand him the case of root beer. I could already envision him saying that I was his beloved son. When I gave him the root beer, he laid it on the counter and never picked it up. He simply said, 'Don't ever waste your money on me." I put my head down and said, "Yes, sir." There is no feeling like being rejected by a parent. He never attended my football, baseball, or basketball games. No matter what achievements. It didn't matter what all-star teams I made it on. No matter what, trophies were presented to me. I couldn't please my stepdad. Finally, I accepted the false narrative that I was a failure of a son. Dysfunctional families can birth terrible tendencies within us. For many years, I bit my nails because I was constantly anxious. Thankfully, God healed me and took the habit away. I had to learn to get affirmation and love from my heavenly father, which became enough for me. The presence of God has to shake off the dysfunction in my life. He began to conform me to his image. The force of his presence overcame the force of my past.

Jacob was forced to try to prove himself to his dad. He was in desperate need of affection. Later, he dressed up like Esau because that was the only way to receive his father's blessing. It was traumatizing. Have you ever experienced something like this with someone you love? No matter what you do, no matter how hard you work, no matter how many gifts you possess, no matter how many achievements you have, that person is just going to say, "I don't care."

There was a force of trauma in the house with Jacob not receiving that love from his father. Jacob had to perform to get his love. He had to work hard, and his actions were fueled by guilt and performance instead of love. The second form of trauma came with his mom. His mom was a manipulator.

Mama manipulated. The word manipulate comes from the Latin words "mani," which means hand, and "pulate," which means to pull or steer. It's when someone uses their hands to steer you in a direction that is not favorable for you but is favorable for them. That's what the word manipulate means. Manipulation is dangerous. The greatest weapon that a manipulator will use on you is guilt. They will try to guilt you into doing what they want. They will make you feel guilty for doing what the Lord wants. Once that weapon is taken out of their hands, they will immediately reach for another weapon called anger. They will try to forcefully bend you to their will with anger. If that doesn't work, they will reach for another weapon called pity/sympathy. They will try to make you feel sorry for them and express how much they need you. If these weapons do not work, they will gossip about you to your friends and family to try to paint you as an evil and selfish person. Their words against you are no match for God's words over you. Be encouraged; they cannot destroy the dream that God has put within you. Be set free from the emotional, spiritual, psychological, and physical bondage. No weapon formed against you shall prosper.

These are the weapons of a manipulator. Rebecca knew how to manipulate things in her favor. Rebekah heard that her husband was about to release the blessing upon Esau, so she devised a masterful plan. She told him to wear Esau's clothes and put goat's hair on his body. She would cook the food and make it taste like it was from Esau.

Rebekah was not thinking of Jacob at this moment; she was thinking of herself. She didn't want Esau to get the birthright because

Esau married Ishmaelites. The Bible states that her daughters-in-law were a constant grief to Rebekah. She could not bear to be around them. If Esau received the birthright, she may have to answer to them. She wanted the son over whom she had influence to receive the birthright. God sovereignly used this for His will to be demonstrated, but we cannot ignore the trauma of manipulation. Rebecca and Jacob deceived Isaac to give Jacob the blessing. Isaac was old and could not see well. They connived to take advantage of a handicapped person. Now, Esau wants to kill Jacob for taking the blessing that belonged to him.

Look at the trauma. Rejection from dad. Manipulation from mom. Hatred and jealousy from the brother. These are all traumatic events that build up. Dysfunction and chaos were reigning in this home. He was born and raised in trauma. This was before he even endured any resistance from outside of the house. It is difficult to deal with negatives on the job, church, and school whenever 18 years of your life was already traumatic. Enduring resistance when you leave the house makes a person feel like they are being targeted. It makes them feel as if they cannot do anything right. It makes you sensitive to criticism, or it makes you a perfectionist, so you do not receive criticism from the outside. But the criticism within you can be sabotaging. You have already been through so much at home that your senses are incredibly sensitive. Any ounce of trauma on the outside will make you just curl up and say, "I quit. I've already been through enough." Some people have been through more in their first 15 years of life than people have been through in 70 years of life because of trauma. Trauma forces you to grow up early. The problem is that the body is still developing. Whenever trauma comes early, it can stunt your growth because you weren't supposed to be exposed to it so soon.

Rebekah's actions did not impact her; they impacted Jacob. No one wanted to kill Rebecca; they wanted to kill Jacob. Jacob is the one who has to deal with the consequences. Jacob has to flee because his brother is envious and jealous of him. Nonstop trauma. He had to flee his family like a fugitive before feeling ready. He had to battle with the trauma of departure. The trauma of leaving something he loved prematurely.

He left the comfort of his home. He traveled many miles to Laban's house. He did not have anywhere to stay. He was alone and sleeping on a rock he used for a pillow. He meets his uncle Laban, who seems like the perfect father figure. He was everything that Isaac wasn't. He spent time with him. He invested in him. He even had Jacob work for him. But Laban was a manipulator, just like his sister Rebekah. He took a particular interest in Jacob because he felt he could profit from him. Jacob feels like he is part of the family, but his guard is down. Laban had a beautiful daughter named Rachel. Jacob wanted to marry Rachel, but Laban said that he would have to work 7 years for her. Jacob thought he had a father figure, but Laban was trying to profit from his gifts and abilities. Jacob did not recognize his gifts. A manipulator will help you see things you didn't know existed in yourself. But the problem is that they will expose it and use it for their own good. They do not want you to recognize the power that you have where you can become independent of them. Jacob worked for 7 years, but it felt like just a few days because of his love for Rachel. Jacob gets to work, and he works for seven years. Jacob approaches his wedding night. The woman that he married has a veil on. Jacob thought he finally got the girl of his dreams, but he awoke that morning and realized that it was Leah, Rachel's sister. He never expected his father figure to connive and trick him in this harmful way. Laban wanted Jacob to work for him forever, so he wanted him to marry both daughters and keep working. Now that's traumatic. It's the trauma of an uncle manipulating and taking advantage for profit. Laban gets blessed because Jacob is working for him. Jacob was working for Laban for 20 years; Laban changed his wages 10 times. He had the trauma from Laban, his uncle. He had the trauma from his father and his mother. He had the trauma of having to leave Laban. Laban chased him and was going to harm him. Laban did not want him to leave, he was too profitable. He's at contention and war with Laban and that contention with his brother. There comes a moment when he is ready to go back because he has a move of God in his life. Jacob went to Bethel and built an altar. Jacob was afraid of Laban and fearful of encountering Esau. What happens when you go through trauma is that there is a paralysis that prevents you from moving forward because you're holding on to the force of the trauma of what happened in the past. After traumatic events, it is difficult to disconnect yourself from everything that has happened to you. Because the trauma and the force of what happened to you is so much greater than anything that you can see in your future. I am writing to someone who has been paralyzed by the force of trauma in your life. It wasn't just the trauma from mama and daddy. It wasn't just the trauma from the brother. It wasn't just the trauma of the uncle. It wasn't just the trauma of departure. How they defined him when he was born was a traumatic experience. They named him Jacob, which means "heel grabber, supplanter, usurper." Even his name was traumatic. Every time they said, "Jacob," they said, "You thief. You supplanter. You liar." That's what his name meant in Hebrew. It wasn't just what he went through, but it was attached to his identity. Have you ever been raised in a setting where people spoke so down to you that brought it on as your own identity?

Even when no trauma is happening to you, your identity is traumatic.

You can't see anything good in yourself. This is important because he has all this trauma in the past, and he is walking around with this identity of Jacob. He's defined because of something that happened before he was even born. Esau was born first, but Jacob in the womb grabbed Esau's foot and tried to pull it back in because he wanted to be born first.

He was defined by that moment. They called him supplanter and usurper. He's walking around with this traumatic identity. When you're walking around with trauma, you can keep on getting yourself engaged in trauma because now you start choosing your relationships based off of your past trauma. Your daddy abandoned you. Now, you find a husband that is going to abandon you. You get into relationships that are going to abandon you. Why did they leave you? Why did they forsake you? Here's why. Because you were looking for character traits that were just like your daddy. Daddy left the family behind. Now, you're attracted to what you are traumatized by. You become attracted to abusive situations. You had a manipulating mom, and she controlled your mind and everything that you did. In your relationships, that is what you look for. You desire women who are controlling. You look for women who make all the decisions for you because you're looking for somebody who's just like your manipulative mama. You are not here to live out everyone else's vision for your life. God has a vision for you. If you want to discover your purpose and identity, the presence of God will direct you.

The trauma continued intensifying because Jacob was defined by the trauma. There comes a point where the angel spoke to him and said, "It's time for you to go. Go back to Bethel. It's time for you to have a new beginning." But Jacob knew that he had to confront the past to possess the future. If you are going forward, you must confront what is behind you. But Jacob was afraid to confront the past. They came to the river, Jabbok. He left his family on one side of the river. He was preparing to confront the past. He knew he would have to face Esau again. Confronting the past, he knew he could not do it alone. He needed an encounter with God. If you are going to confront the trauma of yesterday, you cannot depend on your ability. You cannot depend on your talent. You need an encounter with God. The Bible states that he was left alone. After enduring pain and trauma, being left alone is the scariest place to be. After abuse, it is easy to become very codependent. Nobody wants to be alone because it's when you're alone that the traumatic memories start coming back. You cannot even sit in silence. You got to have music playing all day. If you are silent by yourself, the memories will start coming back. You have to have the TV playing all day. You need some kind of noise playing in the background. You would rather be around chaos than sit in complete silence. You don't want to be alone. You would rather be in an abusive relationship than to be alone. You would rather stay connected to things trying to destroy you than be alone. You would rather walk around with people that are hurting you, rather than be alone. You would rather stay with toxicity. Because of your past, you would rather be abused than be alone. Logically, that does not sound right to you. But for some reason, emotionally, it does sound right to you. You would rather be connected to dysfunction than be alone. You know they are trying to hurt you. They are trying to destroy your kids. They are trying to destroy your family. They are trying to ruin your future. You know that, but you cannot be alone. You say, "Whatever you do, please don't abandon me. Hit me. Punch me. Reject me. Curse me out. But please, don't abandon me." You need a touch from God to discover your value again. There is no moral virtue in enduring abuse. You are not more holy for enduring manipulation and ignoring corruption. Get out of there for your safety. Place some boundaries around your life. God will be with you. God is going to heal you of your abandonment issues. You are worthy to be loved.

Jacob understood that if he was going to address the past trauma, he had to be willing to be alone with God. He had to trust that the force of God's presence would be greater than the force of the trauma." As scientists have studied the effects of trauma, they often describe how trauma literally gets stored in your physical body. Trauma gets stored within the body, but specifically the hips. Emotional trauma gets stored in the hips. The hips bear the weight of much of your trauma. What happens when you get scared? The hips are affected, and you curl up. You go in the fetal position. When someone wants to hit you, you curl up. The stress, the tension, and the trauma are stored right there in the hips.

Whenever Jacob had an encounter with God, God said, "I have got to disjoint the thigh from the hip to release the trauma out of you, and I've got to allow the force of my presence to be greater than the force of your trauma."

For a change, God's presence had to be applied to his life. He wrestled with the angel; the first thing the angel had to do was disconnect the thigh from the hip. Now, the pain of the encounter with God was more significant than the pain of the past. The force of the encounter with God was greater. The force was so great that he walked with a limp for the rest of his life, but the trauma was released. The force of the future was greater than the force of his past. To overcome the past, you need a forceful encounter with God. You need the presence of God to come down in your life and begin to disconnect you from everything that happened to you and launch you into a new anointing.

This is why God had to go to the hips. That's where all his trauma was from the past. All he could remember was the past. It sat there right in his body. When he disconnected the thigh from the hip, he did not think about the pain of the past anymore. He thought about the pain of the supernatural encounter. When you have trauma stored in your hips, you walk very stiffly. But after this encounter with God, Jacob walked with a limp. He was no longer defined by everything that happened to him yesterday. He was defined by what was happening in the future.

After this forceful encounter, he would never look at things the same. His memories were repurposed. The last time he saw Esau, he saw him through the lens of trauma. After his encounter with God, he looked at him through the lens of the presence of God. Jacob told Esau, "I've seen your face as the face of God." His encounter with God was so incredible that he did not hold a grudge of bitterness or unforgiveness against him. He stopped looking at his brother through the lens of his trauma and started looking at him through the lens of his encounter. "God's done such a work in me from the top of my head to the soles of my feet. I feel a force of the future upon me right now, and it's greater than the force of anything that has happened." You'll come out of this better after an encounter with God. You will come out of this with more power after encountering God.

When you study Isaac Newton's law of motion. He said, "When an object is at rest, it says it'll stay there." But he said, "There has to be a force that comes against the object to make it move. An object, when you set it down, it's at rest. To get the object to move, there must be a force greater than the inertia of the object to make it move."

A rock is at rest. But a greater force has the power to make it move. To make something move, you must apply force. You were created in the image of God. God created you in His image. When you were born, God had a destiny for your life. But a force of trauma was applied to you. You are destined, but the force of trauma has been applied to you. The force of trauma has you going backward and away from where you were designed to be. Remember when you felt innocent. Remember how you were before the hell happened in your life? But what happened? The force of trauma knocked you backward. Now, the only thing that can get you back to where you were destined to be is a greater force must be applied to you to send you forward. This is how Jacob started. The trauma from mom, from dad, from uncle, from brother, the trauma of leaving. He is repeatedly knocked backward. The trauma was stored in his hips. But with one encounter with God, the force of God's presence pushed him forward. The force of the future was applied to his life. The force of the future was greater than the force of the past. All of the trauma was released. God is greater than the pain of the past.

God is greater than your trauma. He is greater than your mistakes. He is greater than your fears. He is greater than your doubts. When God applies the pressure, He will restore the years the enemy has tried to take from you. God is going to redeem the time. The weight of his glory is greater than the weight of the past. When Jacob wrestled with that angel, a force was applied to his body. His hip was disjointed. The thigh was pulled out of the hip socket. There had to be an unbalanced force that would bring the object back into its original design. There had to be something greater that would touch his life. Something from the future has to overwhelm the trauma. There had to be a force from the future.

Something had to be applied to him that made him return to the original design but pushed him into something greater. He was not Jacob anymore. He was designed to be Israel. The pressure was applied to his life to become Israel. The force of the future caused him to bring forth the twelve tribes of Israel. The force of God's presence was so great that Judah came out of him. Judah means praise. God will do such a work in your life where the only thing that comes out of you is praise. Judah came out of him. He had such an encounter that it changed everything about his life.

He wasn't dwelling just in mama's house anymore. No. He became a leader. He became a general. He became a patriarch. He had an encounter with God when he was alone. He got positioned for His presence. He needed the force of the future to be greater than the force of the past. He needed the pull of the future to be greater than the pull of the past. God said, "I know you got trauma stored up in those hips, so I am going to allow some brokenness in that spot." This season of brokenness was not designed to destroy you. It's been designed to disconnect you from everything from yesterday and to connect you to the future.

When there's a season of brokenness, it's a season of transformation. Where there's a season of brokenness, it's a season of you going to a new level. Sometimes, you have to go through brokenness to stop being familiar with trauma. Stop being comfortable with being less than what you are called to be. There's something about brokenness that opens up your eyes. There's something about brokenness that says, "You know what? This is the last time I'm going to cry like this." Sometimes, you can only see clearly through tears.

There's something about brokenness that says, "You know what? This is the last day you'll treat me like this." There's something about brokenness that prepares you for a new name and future. You become tired of the cycle. You become weary of repeating everything that has happened. Brokenness forces you to start speaking positively about your life. There is no other way to go but forward.

God wants to bring transformation. He wants to have a forceful encounter with you today. Instead of rehearsing the pain of yesterday, you begin to speak about the power of what happened to you with God. The —the of a new beginning.

The hips control the balance of the body and are essential for equilibrium. Once Jacob's hips were out of joint, he limped for the rest of his life. For the rest of his life, they asked him, "What's your name?" Israel. "How'd you get that?" He responded, "Do you see how I'm walking?" If they asked about his past, there was nothing to talk about. He had a new beginning. Instead of carrying the burden of the past, he was carrying the burden of his destiny. The future was so heavy he limped. But I would rather carry the burden of the future than the past.

Jacob, do you still feel pain for what mom and dad did to you? He responded, "No. This pain right here overwhelms the pain of my memories. Every day, I wake up in pain, but it feels so good because it reminds me that I had a real encounter." He had an encounter with God where his flesh shrunk.

God wants you to have such an encounter with him that your flesh shrinks. Addiction, pride, anger, and so many other things will shrink out of your life. So many things come out of the flesh. But when you have an encounter, he'll begin to cause that flesh to start shrinking.

You want transformation; you need a force greater than your mistake. You want your life to be changed; you need a force greater than what happened to you because your trauma got you moving in the wrong direction, in fear. You need a force applied to you that says, "Greater is He that is in me than He that is in the world." He is greater. When I walk with Him, He keeps applying the pressure to bring me into what He has called me to be. But you need a force from the future that is greater than the force of the past. To deliver Israel, they had to get a greater force. They got all these false gods there, so God had to put his weight on those gods and say, "No. We're bringing fire from heaven. Now, we're bringing hailstones down. Now, we're bringing 10 plagues to teach them false gods the lesson that there's only one God. Pharaoh thinks he's a god. I'm about to show him that he isn't god over anything." Pharaoh is so strong. He says to God, "No," 10 times. But eventually, he capitulated to that pressure. Then, they got destroyed when he changed his mind and tried to go after Him. God applied force. He applied force so that his glory might be seen.

Jesus Christ went through trauma. The cat of nine tails ripped through His body. The trauma of betrayal. The trauma of your close disciples forsaking you. All that trauma forced Him into the future. There was a force of trauma. He went to that cross. He went to that grave, but the force of His Spirit was greater than the force of that grave. The force of the Spirit raised him out of the grave.

The force of His Spirit is greater. Whatever has tried to bury you cannot stop the Spirit of God from raising you up. You are going to get up again. You're going to resurrect. The trauma affects our personality traits. God can change you from the inside out because there are certain traits that we adapt after going through traumatic experiences. I remember because I went through so much trauma in my childhood, I used to say, "Oh, I don't like to travel far. I don't like having fun like that. I like doing this." I thought that was my personality, and I said that for years until God healed me. Whenever God healed me, I said, "I like this stuff. I like traveling, and I like seeing that." Still, my trauma tried to convince me of a personality that wasn't mine, and I had to be healed in order to see the real me.

God can overcome your nature. He can get into your deep-rooted nature, that thing that's been in there for decades. When he puts his presence on it, he can help it obey God's will. Even though everything in you wants to say no, the force of the encounter is so great that it pulls you into a yes.

He wants to have a forceful encounter with you that overcomes the force of the trauma. Trauma directs you. Trauma directs your steps. Fear will try to control you and make you fearful of God. That's why some people are scared to really have a relationship with God, because God is our father, and you didn't have the most excellent earthly representation of a father. You were scared of your dad, so you tense up when you say that God is a Heavenly Father. You go into freeze. You go into a paralysis. You go into hiding. But if we allow God's presence to come upon us today, if we will yield, everyone says, "Yield." If we surrender to him, we allow him to make a change and a lasting impact that will direct us all of our days. For now, it's about what he has done in you more than anything done to you.

God is going to do something special in your life, and although trauma, abuse, and offense tried to knock you off course. An encounter with God is going to change everything. You are carrying failures and mistakes. Let the force of his love put you back on course. People say, "Well, I feel unworthy." In the Old Testament, "worth" was a business term. It would have scales where you would put gold and silver and shekels where it was a balance. But when the balance was equal, it was called it's of equal worth. It was worth it. It was worthy.

When one doesn't have enough, then the scale becomes unworthy. You may feel unworthy, but the word "glory" literally means to ascribe weight to something. God has a weight to him. His glory is weighty. When he puts his glory on you. When he puts his presence on you. His name and his blood make you worthy. When you feel unworthy, all you have to say is, "Worthy is the lamb." What he did on the cross for you makes you worthy. The force of his blood is greater than the force of my mistake.

Disconnect me from the trauma, heartache, and anything that's happened. God will place his glory upon you, which will outweigh the trauma. The force of the future is greater than the force of the abuse. If sin can destroy a life, then his grace can save a life. The force of sin is no match for the force of grace. Where sin did abound, grace doth much more abound. Through the grace of God, you are moving forward.

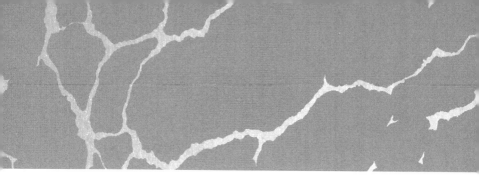

Forgive the person that hurt you. Forgive the person who thinks that they haven't done anything wrong. Forgive the person who refuses to ask for forgiveness. Forgiveness may not always lead to reconciliation with them, but forgiveness will always lead you to deliverance. Let go of anger, deception, and bitterness. God will heal you. Move on. God has better things in store for you.

8

THE BONES OF A DREAMER

*"And the bones of Joseph, which the children of Israel
brought up out of Egypt, buried they in Shechem, in a
parcel of ground which Jacob bought of the sons of Hamor
the father of Shechem for an hundred pieces of silver: and
it became the inheritance of the children of Joseph."*

JOSHUA 24:32 KJV

Something about Joseph's life puts us in touch with the potential of a dream. "Where there is no vision, the people perish. He that keepeth the law, happy is he." One translation says, "Where there is no dream, the people cast off restraint." Meaning there's no need for discipline if there is no dream. Where there is no dream, there is no discipline. If there is no dream, it is easy to fall prey to past failures, betrayals, and the hurts of yesterday. If you do not have anything to pull you forward, then what is behind you will try to pull you backward.

If you don't have a vision for tomorrow, then yesterday will try to lay hold on you and pull you back into what was. But you cannot do anything with what was. You can only do something with what you have today for your future. To help you overcome your history, God will put a dream on the inside of you. The dream will ignite you to go forward. The presence of a dream helps you to put the past behind you. The dream allows you to realize that you are not defined by the failures of yesterday. It's time to stop putting your energy into the pain of what happened and start getting on board with the dream and what is about to happen.

Your future is greater than your past. What is ahead of you is greater than what is behind you. Joseph is the greatest dreamer in the Old Testament, but his life is filled with hell. What a paradox. Dreams are supposed to be beautiful. You thought the dream was supposed to have you starry-eyed. But after the dream comes, that's when the tears come. Why? The tears help you see your dream more clearly. Something about looking through the lens of a tear that puts the focus more on the dream. There is something about tears that helps magnify the dream.

Tears are a part of the healing process of letting go. Those who hold on to the past feel ashamed for crying. You must allow the healthy tears to release from their body because it's a sign that you are putting the pain behind you and going forward. When you cry, healing hormones are released. What has been boiling within you is finally released through tears. It takes strength to cry. Tears are necessary to go forward. You are no longer crying over what happened; you are crying to go forward. You are crying with gratefulness. The trial does not stop the dream. The tears are a sign that you are going forward.

Joseph was dead for nearly 500 years, and his bones were finally buried. It is a peculiar place where they were buried in the promised land. His bones were buried in Shechem. They could have buried Joseph's bones anywhere in the promised land. Why did they choose Shechem? Shechem is the one place on earth where his bones shouldn't be buried. Because Shechem is the place where all the hell in his life started.

500 years earlier, his bones were buried in Shechem. Shechem was the place where all the hell broke loose in his family. It was in Shechem that his older sister was raped. Dinah was raped and taken advantage of in Shechem.

"And Dinah the daughter of Leah, which she bare unto Jacob, went out to see the daughters of the land. And when Shechem the son of Hamor the Hivite, prince of the country, saw her, he took her, and lay with her, and defiled her (Genesis 34:1-2 KJV).

It was in this terrible city that the prince of Shechem defiled Dinah. This place was a place filled with rape. After Simeon and Levi, Joseph's brothers heard about this rape, they wanted revenge upon the people of Shechem. They devised a plan and took matters into their own hands. Fueled by revenge, they killed all the men in Shechem. So Shechem was a place of rape. It was a place of trauma. It was a place of murder. It was a place that Joseph wanted to forget because that's where all the hell started in his family. Everybody was getting along until there was Shechem. Everything changed in Shechem. Rape. Murder. Trauma. Revenge. Shechem was a place that they wanted to forget. This was a place that you wanted to put behind you. This was a place that you didn't want any part to deal with. But later, Joseph's bones would be buried in Shechem. What a mystery.

"Now Israel loved Joseph more than all his children, because he was the son of his old age: and he made him a coat of many colours. And when his brethren saw that their father loved him more than all his brethren, they hated him, and could not speak peaceably unto him. And Joseph dreamed a dream, and he told it his brethren: and they hated him yet the more (Genesis 37:3-5 KJV).

They hated him, but guess where the trouble really started? Shechem.

"And his brethren envied him; but his father observed the

saying. And his brethren went to feed their father's flock in Shechem. And Israel said unto Joseph, Do not thy brethren feed the flock in Shechem? come, and I will send thee unto them. And he said to him, Here am I. And he said to him, Go, I pray thee, see whether it be well with thy brethren, and well with the flocks; and bring me word again. So he sent him out of the vale of Hebron, and he came to Shechem" (Genesis 37:11-14).

Not only was this a place of rape and murder, and trauma, but the father was afraid of his sons being in Shechem because of the trouble that they had previously caused. He told Joseph to check on his brothers to ensure there would be no more mischief. Whenever he went towards Shechem, he never returned home. In Shechem, a conspiracy was being built against Joseph. Before Shechem, the brother's envy towards him was passive. They did not like him, but they refused to act against him. But after Shechem, his envy for him turned into active envy. Perhaps the spirit of revenge and bloodlust had not sufficiently been quenched with the death of the men of Shechem. Joseph searched for his brothers in Shechem and couldn't find them. They told Joseph that his brothers had gone on to Dothan. The brothers were already conspiring to get rid of him. Nobody wanted to be connected to Shechem. It was a place of rape. It was a place of murder. It was a place of conspiracy. Nobody wants to be aligned with Shechem. Joseph is thrown into the pit. He is lied on in Potiphar's house. He is falsely accused and thrown into prison. But he does not let go of his dream. He was defined by his dream. His brothers did not even call Joseph by his name when they betrayed him. They said, "Behold, this dreamer is coming." The dream defined his life.

Joseph went to the pit, Potiphar's house, and the prison. Finally, after interpreting Pharoah's dreams, he became Pharoah's second in command. He had children, and he became second in command to Pharoah. He received the keys to the storehouse. He saved Egypt and his family from the famine. He forgives his family.

> *"And Joseph said unto his brethren, I die: and God will surely visit you, and bring you out of this land unto the land which he sware to Abraham, to Isaac, and to Jacob. And Joseph took an oath of the children of Israel, saying, God will surely visit you, and ye shall carry up my bones from hence"* (Genesis 50:24-25 KJV).

Joseph said, "I know that I am in Egypt, but my bones do not belong in Egypt. I do not only have a dream where I'm second in command to Pharoah. I dream my bones will be buried in the promised land for an inheritance."

Even though his eyes did not see the promised land, his bones did. The dream in his mind, heart, and soul had saturated his life right down to his bones. The dream did not end with him being in Egypt; his dream was also for his lineage to enter the promised land. 430 years later, Moses took up the bones of Joseph and brought them with him whenever they departed Egypt.

> *"But God led the people about, through the way of the wilderness of the Red sea: and the children of Israel went up harnessed out of the land of Egypt. And Moses took the bones of Joseph with him: for he had straitly sworn the children of Israel, saying, God will surely visit you; and ye shall carry up my bones away hence with you* (Exodus 13:18-19 KJV).

Moses took up Joseph's bones and brought them with them through-out the wilderness. Those bones were looking for a place to stay. They carried Joseph's bones for 40 years. They would not bury them until they came into the promise. After almost 500 years, they buried Joseph's bones in Shechem. The place of his trauma became the place of his inheritance. His bones were buried in the place where the rape, murder, trauma, and conspiracy. Essentially, Joseph said, "When you bury my bones, bury them in the place that you thought I was defined by. You thought I was defined by the rape, the murder, and the trauma. No, it's going to become my inheritance. I want you to put my bones there because I want you to know that what I went through did not defeat me." Wow. The place that was the place of pain became the place of promise. What he went through did not defeat him. He took dominion over what was trying to defeat him. He was not defined by the hell. He was defined by the dream. They put his bones in that place where they thought he would run away from forever. But when his bones were brought back to that place, his bones came back with dominion. This was a testament in Scripture that he was not defined by what he went through. He was defined by the dream that God gave him. His dream outlived him. The same place where the hell happened is where the dream occurred. Some-body who's been running away from your past as if your past has the final say over you. But God has put a dream inside of you. No rape. No hurt. No traumatic event can destroy the dream God has put into your bones. You are going to be buried in the promised land. You're not defined by what happened.

The children of Israel buried his bones in the place of trauma. After all that you have been through, you still have trauma triggers. You've been holding on to the betrayal. I know you still have the knife in your back from being backstabbed. You cover the wounds as best you can, but the blood seeps through your clothes. You have been through so much hell. A band-aid cannot cover this level of pain. With what you have been through, it is obvious that you have been to Shechem.

You have gone through some type of hurt. You have gone through some kind of abuse. Friends turned their back on you and left you for dead. They threw you in a pit. I don't know if it was your dad that left you. I don't know if it was your mama that walked out. I don't know if it was a best friend that hurt you. All I know is I'm writing to people living in Shechem. But you are not going to be defined by the trauma. You will be defined by the dream placed in your bones. It is not defined by the bruises but by the bones. Hell is not going to destroy you. The dream has the final say over your life. The same place where the destruction started became a place of his inheritance. What belonged to the devil, belonged to God now. What belonged to the trauma belonged to God now. What belonged to the loss belonged to the dream now. It's time for you to regain the joy you lost in Shechem. It's time to get back to regain the peace that you lost in Shechem. It's time to get back the anointing that you lost in Shechem. It belongs to you. Your trauma has been holding onto it for too long. I've come to tell the devil it's time to let my people go. It's time to let the dream go. It's time to let the anointing go.

I'm writing to people who have been unable to move on from the place of Shechem because every time you close your eyes to go to sleep, you think about the situation and the traumatic event that occurred. It has been a bad memory since you went to that place in your life. You know more about the past than you do your own future.

After you go through a season of depression, anxiety, postpartum, or betrayal, you can see if someone else is struggling with that same issue. After you survive and overcome that season, God puts dominion within you. God has given you dominion over what has tried to destroy you. You survived the storm, and now you are equipped. My wife had a battle with postpartum depression after my son was born in 2016. I remember the day that she visited her personal Shechem. It was a challenging time in our lives. Her anxiety was through the roof. She was usually very happy and joyful, but she would be anxious for no reason. I felt helpless because no matter how I tried to help she wasn't getting any better. She wrestled with this for about a year. She truly is a fantastic wife and mother. She overcame that season of depression and anxiety. Afterward, God gave her special authority over depression and anxiety. She can see whenever other women are battling these things, and she can powerfully minister to them. She defeated these things in her own life, and now she helps women to defeat them in their lives.

That's what happened with David whenever he battled Goliath; when he battled Goliath, he ran and walked into that battle with just a stone and a sling. He killed Goliath. But after he hit Goliath down, he didn't just want to win. He wanted to be more than a conqueror. He took the sword out of the enemy's hand and killed his enemy with his sword. You see, he had dominion over what he went through. We don't just win a battle but come out with new tools after the battle. We don't just win the war, but we come out with new weapons from the war.

We are more than conquerors. We overcome by the blood of the lamb and the word of our testimony. The blood is enough, but God wants you to be more than a conqueror. He wants you to start testifying. God always causes us to triumph. A triumph was the highest form of honor in Rome. Roman generals would bring the slaves and trophies in front of people to celebrate the spoils of war. It was similar to a championship parade. When God triumphs. He brings depression, fear, and anxiety in chains behind him. He defeated these things. Thanks be to God, which always causes us to triumph. He defeated it so that we could defeat it. He led captivity captive.

Now, the enemy tried to defeat you with depression, but now you have dominion over depression. You have authority over that spirit that's been tormenting you.

Why? Because you have lost the dream. You stopped believing in God's word over your life. You stopped believing in the dream that God gave you in His presence. You have looked at the adverse situation of being in Shechem and thought it robbed you of your destiny and anointing. But the dream will still come to pass. It's time to let it go. It is time to inherit what's rightfully yours.

After you get born again of the water and the Spirit, the sin is gone. But the memories remain. How do I deal with the past hell while also embracing a future? How do I deal with the trauma and still embrace the triumph? There is a tug of war. It is like this pendulum that shifts. One day, you're good, and you are in the land of promise. But another day, you go back to the land of the trauma. There's something about those trauma triggers that can set you back for weeks and months.

Someone says or does something, and it gets you back right where you started. God wants to give you a dream that outweighs the past trauma. The future is going to be greater than the trauma of the past. It's time to forget those things that are behind and reach forth into those things that are before. It's time to press toward the mark of the high calling in Jesus Christ.

It's time to say, "Get thee behind me, Satan. I'm going where God told me I would go. Get thee behind me, Shechem. I'm going where God told me I would go." Shechem is where your worst memories are. The only way to conquer those memories is to allow your dream to conquer that thing. It doesn't define me. You cannot ignore Shechem, you have to conquer it. It doesn't define me. God not only wants you to learn how to get over the trauma. He wants you to let your trauma know that it does not own you. You own the trauma. Your trauma does not create the narrative in your life; you make the narrative. Your trauma doesn't own you. You own it. Your dream will still be fulfilled despite it. Yes, the trauma happened. But I want my bones to be buried there to send a message to the enemy. I am not ashamed of what I went through. I am not going to delete my history. I am going to repurpose it for the glory of God. A little leaven leavens the whole lump, and God said the kingdom is as a leaven. It's like a leaven, putting it into some bread, and, over time, it starts taking over the whole bread. He does the change from the inside out. We want Him to eliminate the memories, but he wants us to see our memories through the lens of his Spirit. He is giving you a new vision, not through the lens of yesterday. But through the lens of His glory. He won't take away the memories because he wants you to process them through the lens of a dream.

You have been through so much in Shechem that you will not tolerate Shechem's behavior in the future. When you are in a tense situation, you can handle it better than others because you have already been to Shechem. Others give up. Not you because you have already been to Shechem. People try to intimidate you, but they can't because you have already been through hell. There is nothing you can threaten you with. You have authority over your experience. You see your experience through a different lens. Although you were a victim, you do not have a victim mentality. When others visit Shechem, they don't interpret it as the land where the trauma happened. They visit Shechem to see Joseph's bones. They visit to see where a dreamer outlived the trauma. You outlived the trauma. You're still here. Hell took his best shot against you in Shechem, but you are worshiping God while reading this book. Joseph inherited a place that he didn't even know that he would inherit. Joseph didn't know that the next time he returned to Shechem, he would return as an owner. The dream outlived him. The dream was more significant than the trauma. The trauma did not last, but the dream did. When you think of Joseph's story, no one ever talks about Shechem. But everyone talks about the dream.

Your dream is greater than the trauma. What's coming for you is greater than anything that you have been through.

If you continue looking at the future through the lens of yesterday, you will have a skewed view. You won't really understand what God is trying to do. God is trying to open the door, but you lock it and run away fearful. Why? Because when you see doors, you freeze and panic. Why? Because the last door that you walked through, they hurt you. God is trying to open up a door of blessing, but you're seeing it through a past lens. Therefore, you cannot step in because you continue processing the blessing before you through the lens of the pain behind you.

You are going to have to stop thinking about what happened in Shechem. You'll have to start thinking about what God put down in your bones. You have to start thinking about the dream in your bones.

Some say, "I come to serve notice to the devil." I didn't come to serve notice to the devil. I've come to show up unannounced. I didn't come to give the devil an eviction notice. I've come to kick open the door and say, "Devil, you should have never touched their kids. You should have never touched their family. You should have never touched their marriage. You should have never touched their ministry."

Joseph said, "You can take my coat but can't take my dream. You can take my coat, but you can't take my bones." The enemy has to leave the bones behind because the bones are going to inherit everything that you thought you lost. The enemy thought your future would be in this pit, but your dream got you out. You thought your future would be in Potiphar's house, but your dream got you out of it. The enemy thought your future would be in prison, but your dream got you out of it. You thought your future would be in the palace, but your dream said, "I'm bringing you out of it because this palace is sooner or later going to turn into slavery. You are not even designed to be there forever."

The dream that God is giving you is going to outlive the pit. It's going to outlive the prison. It's going to outlive Egypt, and it's going to find a place in the Promised Land.

Jesus robed himself in the flesh because He had a dream. He had a dream in His Spirit. He had a dream down in His bones. He came to the earth and walked for 33 years trying to multiply the dream. The dream was a part of every fiber of his being. His dream was all the way down in His bones. Judas did not believe in the dream. Judas betrayed him in Gethsemane. They whipped Jesus' body, but he wouldn't let go of his dream. He had the dream down in His bones. They nailed him to the cross. But he would not let go of this dream.

The Romans wanted to make sure that the people on the cross were dead. The custom was that they would break the legs of those on the cross with a hammer to ensure their death. They broke the bones of the thief on the right. Then they broke the bones of the thief on the left. But when they came to Jesus, they refused to break his bones. There was a prophecy that not one of his bones would be broken. They broke the bones of the other thief, but they came to Jesus, and there was a prophecy that not one of His bones would be broken.

They could take his life on the cross, but they couldn't take the bones away. He had the bones of a dreamer. They had to leave the bones behind because he was going to walk in his resurrected body three days later. He walked among them for 40 days in his resurrected body. They took his sleep. Took his crown of thorns. Tore his body. They let his blood flow out on the ground. But they had to leave the bones behind. He had the bones of a dreamer. The dream outlived the hell. The dream outlived Calvary. The dream outlived the betrayal. He had the bones of a dreamer.

You have the bones of a dreamer. You've got to get this dream down in your bones no matter how much hell you go through.

The Bible says they went up to the upper room, and while they began to eat, he said, "One of you shall betray me." The Bible says something started to shake in that atmosphere, and they were fearful because it sent a chill down to their bones. Somebody's going to deny Jesus. Somebody's going to betray Jesus in that upper room. But after that moment, he went to the cross, was resurrected, and was seen by them for 40 days. The Bible says they went to the upper room on the day of Pentecost and to that same upper room where they prophesied his death.

There is geographical, theological, and historical significance to that upper room. The same upper room where it was all about death and betrayal. That same upper room was where the Holy Spirit was poured out in Acts 2. Jesus did not leave his bones behind but left his Spirit behind. With the Spirit of Christ, you will overcome every trauma. Every form of abuse. Every offense. You have the bones of a dreamer. You have the Spirit of a dreamer. Hold on to the dream. Don't you let go. Do not give up. Don't throw in the towel? Don't hurt yourself. God is not done with you.

I feel chains beginning to break off of you while reading. You are holding on to God and letting go of the past. You are letting go of the insecurities. You are letting go of the toxicity, and I'm going forward. Thank God you survived the hell. Thank God you survived yesterday. Thank God you survived the trauma, but you didn't survive just to survive. You survived so you can thrive. Don't you bury my bones in Egypt. You bring me back to the hell. You bring me back to the trouble. You bring me back to the trouble, and I will not be defeated by what happened. You will defeat what has tried to defeat you. You will conquer what has tried to conquer you. You will overcome because Jesus overcame for you. Share your story with someone. Through your pain, you found philanthropy. Through your bruises, you found your burden. You have the bones of a dreamer. You have been placed upon this earth for a reason. Share your story. Testify. Declare. Love. You win in this chapter. Everything changes here. Your story is just getting started.

ABOUT THE AUTHOR

Pastor Victor Jackson is the founder and Senior Pastor of the Bible Center of Orlando. He is also the founder and Bishop of the Bible Center churches. He is a Best-Selling author; his book "A Word to the Broken" has touched thousands of lives and is used by renowned therapists around the United States to assist people on the path of healing and victory. Victor M. Jackson has a Bachelor's in Interdisciplinary Studies, a Master's in Theological Studies, and a Master's in Biblical Exposition. Pastor Jackson is currently a PhD student in Bible Exposition & Christian Leadership. He is a renowned conference speaker, and his sermons have touched millions. He has a heart for people and models a life of sacrifice that continues to impact leaders worldwide. He hosts a popular podcast, "Bible Centered with Victor Jackson." Pastor Jackson and his wife Luisa have two children, James Asher and Mia Victoria. They love doing ministry together as a family. They are constantly searching for ways to meet the needs of their community and beyond.

Made in the USA
Monee, IL
19 November 2024

70653222R00102